suddenly single mom

52 MESSAGES
OF HOPE, GRACE, AND PROMISE

JEANETTE HANSCOME

Jeanette Hanscome shares 52 encouraging insights gleaned from her first year as a single mom to two boys. Her very real struggles and triumphs will help you as you determine when to stand on your own and when to ask for or accept help. Jeanette's book is a worthy companion to anyone who is now a single mother.

Su   ls like

a   you a

cu   *there.*

And then, when you're ready, she shares some of her hard-won wisdom, a little at a time, to help you to uncover the unexpected lessons and blessings in your own journey. Encouraging, empowering, hopeful, and wise.

Susy Flory, a *New York Times* bestselling author
and director of the West Coast Christian Writers Conference

Suddenly Single Mom is a true, sustaining respite in the midst of the craziness of life. Jeanette Hanscome becomes both wise mentor and empathetic friend through the tumultuous journey called single motherhood. Biblical, honest, and hopeful, this devotional will surely refresh every single mom who reads it.

Mary DeMuth, author of *Worth Living:
How God's Wild Love for You Changes Everything*

With refreshing authenticity and openness, Jeanette Hanscome welcomes you into her world as a single mom and offers you hope and encouragement for yours. In this gem of a book, you will find relatable stories, practical tips, and a caring friend in Jeanette to come alongside you on your journey. This will be the book you'll want to keep on your nightstand to dip into again and again.

Judy Gordon Morrow, author of
The Listening Heart: Hearing God in Prayer

Suddenly is not an easy word. It signals abruptness. Hastiness. Shock. And when it's applied to something as vital as going from being half of a mother—father family to being an on-her-own single mom, it sounds . . . well, in author Jeanette Hanscome's words, devastating. Hopeless. Heartbreaking. In 52 messages, each based on scripture, built around personal experience, and peppered with hard-won insights, Jeanette leads readers toward hope and peace and healing through God's grace. I especially like the survival tips at the end of each message. Good job, Jeanette. Countless suddenly single moms will thank you for this work from your heart.

Kay Marshall Strom, author and speaker

We never need God more than when life throws a crushing curve. Through devotions based on her personal story, Jeanette, a visually impaired woman who suddenly finds herself as a single mom, shows us that what changes us forever does not have to ruin or define our future.

Marci Seither, author of
Empty Nest: Strategies to Help Your Kids Take Flight

Suddenly Single Mom is a gift for women who desperately need to know they are not alone. Through her transparent writing, Jeanette takes readers on a journey from "How will I survive this?" to seeing God's power at work. As someone who's been a single mom, I know the power of encouragement when you feel alone. *Suddenly Single Mom* is that desperately needed encouragement a mom needs.

Kathi Lipp, speaker and author of fifteen books,
including *Clutter Free*

When we said "I do" few of us expected our marriage would later end in divorce. But that's a painful reality many of us were forced to face. When children are involved, the pain is almost unbearable. Jeanette Hanscome's *Suddenly Single Mom* is a vulnerable and wise companion for the woman who finds herself facing that harsh reality. Jeanette shares from her own experience and from her heart, offering herself to single mothers as both guide and friend. Ultimately, this is a book that will draw single mom's into a deeper intimacy with their One True Love, Jesus Christ.

Ginny L. Yttrup, award-winning author of *Words*

suddenly
single
mom

52 MESSAGES
OF HOPE, GRACE, AND PROMISE

JEANETTE HANSCOME

WORTHY*
Inspired

Published by Worthy Inspired, an imprint of Worthy Publishing Group, a division of Worthy Media, Inc., One Franklin Park, 6100 Tower Circle, Suite 210, Franklin, TN 37067.

WORTHY is a registered trademark of Worthy Media, Inc.

HELPING PEOPLE EXPERIENCE THE HEART OF GOD

Library of Congress Cataloging-in-Publication Data

Names: Hanscome, Jeanette, author.
Title: Suddenly single mom : 52 messages of hope, grace, and promise / Jeanette Hanscome.
Description: Franklin, TN : Worthy Publishing, 2016.
Identifiers: LCCN 2015051055 | ISBN 9781617956676 (tradepaper)
Subjects: LCSH: Single mothers--Religious life. | Motherhood--Religious aspects--Christianity.
Classification: LCC BV4529.18 .H36 2016 | DDC 204/.41--dc23
LC record available at http://lccn.loc.gov/2015051055

All Scripture quotations, unless otherwise indicated, are taken from THE HOLY BIBLE, NEW INTERNATIONAL VERSION®, NIV® Copyright © 1973, 1978, 1984, 2011 by Biblica, Inc.® Used by permission. All rights reserved worldwide. | Scripture quotations marked NKJV are taken from the New King James Version. Copyright © 1982 by Thomas Nelson, Inc. Used by permission. All rights reserved. | Scripture quotations marked NASB are taken from the New American Standard Bible®. Copyright © 1960, 1962, 1963, 1968, 1971, 1972, 1973, 1975, 1977, 1995 by The Lockman Foundation. Used by permission. | Scripture quotations marked NLT are taken from the Holy Bible, New Living Translation, Copyright © 2007. Used by permission of Tyndale House Publishers, Inc., Wheaton, Illinois 60189. All rights reserved.

ISBN: 978-1-61795-667-6

Cover Design: Kent Jensen
Cover Illustration: Getty Images

Printed in the United States of America
16 17 18 19 20 WOR 10 9 8 7 6 5 4 3 2 1

For Christian and Nathan,
two of God's most precious gifts to me

Contents

Section 3: Preventing an Emotional Wreck

Section 4: Finding My Way

Section 5: Time to Start Over

Section 6: A Beautiful Thing

Note to Readers

ONE CHALLENGE of writing a book for single moms was authentically communicating the truth of my experience while respecting my former husband. Regardless of how his choices impacted my life, I wanted to honor the fact that he is still the father of my two sons. He has a family, a job, and friends, and I have forgiven him. For this reason, I decided not to use his name, include details about the issues that ended our marriage, or reveal where we lived.

My hope is that you will not think less of him or anyone else, but will see God's grace at work in painful circumstances as you walk through your own journey.

Introduction

WHEN I FELT THE TUG to write a devotional for single moms, I didn't think I had any business doing it. One of my sons was already a young adult (still living at home) when my husband left. By the time I started outlining the book, my youngest son and I had moved in with my parents. Unlike some single moms, I had a strong support system from the very first day.

"I hardly think I'm living the typical single-mom experience," I told a friend.

"But you're living *your* story," she insisted. "Look what God has done."

Her response reminded me that I had something unique to offer—my experience as a single mom who is also visually impaired took me to a new level of dependency on God and others. My experience continues to be a lesson in His ability to equip us for what feels impossible.

Your story might be very different from mine. But certain things are consistent regardless of the details:

Adjusting to the single-mom life is exhausting, painful, and hard.

Divorce and all that comes with it makes it even harder.

The stress and grief can bring out our worst and our best.

It changes everything—our dreams, our relationships, and us.

We need Jesus more than ever.

It takes a long time to accept, make sense of, and feel at home in this new life.

My prayer is that you will find hope, strength, and healing in each of these devotions and be moved to cling to your heavenly Father during this time of loss, change, and transition.

Each chapter includes a piece of my personal story, a Scripture passage, a thought to consider as you go into your day or week, a prayer, and a practical survival tip. If you are a lover of journals like I am, this would be a great time to start a fresh one. I still treasure those I kept. If you've never been one to write down your thoughts and feelings, I encourage you to give it try. Consider it a record of God's work as you draw close to the One who will never abandon you.

As hard as it is to carve out time for yourself right now, or even focus for very long, consider these short readings permission to pull away for a few moments and draw on the love, grace, and hope that only a perfect heavenly Father can provide.

SECTION 1

suddenly single

1

Moving

I would have despaired unless I had believed that I would see the goodness of the LORD in the land of the living.

Psalm 27:13 NASB

I SHOULD HAVE KNOWN BETTER than to check e-mail on vacation. My younger son, Nathan, and I were celebrating my mom's birthday with a family trip to Disneyland. Outside the Magic Kingdom, life had temporarily turned upside down. While everyone wound down from a fun-filled day, I scanned my in-box for anything important before checking in with my twenty-year-old, Christian, who'd stayed home.

My heart froze when I saw a message from my husband. Subject: *Moving.*

He had accepted a job in a town several hours from our home. He no longer wanted to be married.

I saw it coming, but his words still felt like a punch in the stomach. Two months earlier, after a year of attempting to confront some serious issues, I had agreed to a trial separation, but I remained committed to restoring our marriage. Apparently restoration wouldn't be happening.

As I reread his message, I sent my emotions into lockdown, determined not to ruin everyone else's fun. I would not hit my nine-year-old with this news during a Disneyland trip with his grandparents, aunt, and cousins.

I was on my way to being a divorced woman after twenty-two and a half years of marriage.

After two months of going it alone "for a while," I had become a single mom for good.

As a woman who has been legally blind since birth and can't drive, I was literally stranded. From that night on, I would be dependent on my church, friends, family, and God. I had no idea if my husband would continue to be part of his sons' lives or disappear. I didn't know if we would be able to keep our house or if I would have to trade freelance writing and editing for a full-time job. Would my friends support me or pull away? Would I end up on welfare? All I knew was life would never be the same.

There is something about being thrown onto God's mercy that awakens either a desire to give up or a refusal to let the unwanted twists lick us. As I reflect back on that heart-numbing night and all the pain that followed, I see it as a journey filled with God's closeness and grace. As I relive the shock of abandonment, I recognize the determination that bubbled up with the devastation. Somehow I knew that this would change me forever but not destroy me—that this time of indescribable loss would end with me seeing God's goodness.

"I would have despaired unless I had believed that I would see the goodness of the LORD in the land of the living" (NASB). The words of Psalm 27:13 became my reason to not give in to hopelessness no matter how bleak my situation looked, and on that night in my hotel bedroom, it looked pretty bad. Even then, God's goodness shone. He'd allowed me to get the news while surrounded by family and being refreshed by a vacation before facing a long process that I never imagined being part of.

If you are reading this book, you have also experienced a moment that changed everything—a phone call, a discovery, a choice, a heartbreaking talk that hurtled you into the life you are in now. Maybe you're still reeling from the blow, wondering how you will survive. Maybe you made the difficult choice to end your marriage because you knew that was best for you and your children. Wherever you are, allow the words of Psalm 27:13 to fill you with hope and strength as you navigate your new life, grieve what is lost, and help your kids make sense of what they can't understand.

May you move through this day with the One who promises to be with you through the uncertainty, make your tears count for something, and allow you to see His goodness in the land of the living.

God, I know You are with me. Right now all I can see are crumbled pieces of what was once my life. I have no idea what lies ahead, except that Your Word promises that I will eventually see Your goodness. Let me see a tiny glimpse of it today as I learn to trust You in a deeper way. Amen.

TO TAKE INTO YOUR DAY

Read: Psalm 27

Consider: What gives you hope that you will see God's goodness, even in these difficult circumstances? How has He been good already?

Survival Tip: Buy a journal especially for tracking God's faithfulness to you.

2

So This Is My Life

I can do all this through him who gives me strength.

Philippians 4:13

ANNE GAVE ME A HUG before we headed to our favorite coffee shop. "I found you a ride to Craft Night."

Anne's kids-welcome Craft Nights provided a dose of fellowship and an escape from the reality of my uncertain future.

"Kelly offered to pick you up. Her son goes to school with our kids. She's a single mom, extremely sweet . . ."

A single mom. Why do I feel like that's supposed to be significant?

Then it hit me.

Oh yeah, I'm a single mom too.

I still had to remind myself that I'd entered a new demographic. A few days earlier, I'd read a blog post that slammed single parents. The anger it stirred shocked me. *Hey, she's talking about me!* In a rare moment of boldness, I stood up for those of us who were doing our best under difficult circumstances.

There in Anne's car, I had to remind myself again. *I'm a single mom.*

I was now a woman whom some would pity or make assumptions about. Others would call me courageous. I would start saying things like, "He's visiting his dad this weekend" and "My attorney says . . ." I had joined the world of child support payments and custody agreements.

I had no idea how Kelly became a single mom, but I knew how I got there, and it stunk.

But there I sat with Anne, who represented a growing circle of support. Knowing my sweet friend, she had been strategic when arranging for Kelly to pick me up for Craft Night.

Kelly arrived on Friday evening. While our boys talked in the backseat, I got to know a wonderful woman who was devoted to her son. Though Kelly and I never became close friends, I caught myself observing her from afar, learning from her example of strength and perseverance.

A few of my older friends had once been single moms. Their stories and words of wisdom became lifelines as I learned to navigate this new life. I also encountered bitter mothers who huddled in the bleachers during Little League games, bashing their exes and comparing complaints. *I don't ever want to sound that sour and ugly.*

All of these examples, good and not-so-pretty, showed me that I would be a lot more successful if I asked God to help me accept my new status. Whether I wanted it or not, this was my life, so what kind of single mom did I want to be?

I wanted to be the one clinging to God and making the best of a sad situation, a woman who defied the statistics and might even cause an opinionated blogger to rethink her snap judgments.

I could not do any of that alone. I needed sensitive friends like Anne and good examples like Kelly. Most of all, I needed God, and the assurance of my heavenly Father, who loved me regardless of my label long before I realized, *Oh yeah, I'm a single mom.*

———

Becoming a single parent means realizing that certain statistics, phrases, and check boxes now apply to us.

While we try to be the best mothers that we know how to be under trying circumstances, we can draw comfort from the knowledge that we aren't in this alone. God has beautiful ways of sending women into our lives who show us the truth in Philippians 4:13: "I can do all this through him who gives me strength."

As you adjust to *I'm a single mom*, and learn to say that dreaded phrase out loud, look to the Father, who saw this stage of your life coming, loves you regardless of what anyone else says or assumes, and is waiting for you to call on Him for help. He alone can mold you into the kind of mom you want to be from this day on.

Lord, I'm a single mom. I never expected to be. Help me accept my new life even if I don't like it. Melt my resentment so I don't become bitter. Help me today to do the best job I can, and to draw on Your strength every moment. Amen.

TO TAKE INTO YOUR DAY

Read: Isaiah 30:19–21

Consider: What kind of mom do you want to be? What kind of mom do you *not* want to become?

Survival Tip: Ask God to send someone you can look to for a good example, support, and prayer as you adjust to your new life.

3

Protecting His Heart

Give me a sign of your goodness . . .

Psalm 86:17

I DON'T REMEMBER exactly how or when I broke the news to Christian and Nathan that "Dad needs to leave for a while" had changed to "Dad isn't coming home." But I do remember in vivid detail the afternoon when Nathan asked one of those questions that stops a newly solo parent's heart.

We were sitting at the kitchen table, Nathan doing homework and me making a grocery list. He still had his school uniform on. Nathan looked up. "Mom, am I going to start doing that thing where I'm with you half the week and Dad half the week?"

God, no, I'm not ready for this discussion.

But it was probably long overdue. His friend Jake split time between his mom's house and dad's.

How do I explain? He is going to be crushed.

The truth was I had no idea how often Nathan would see his dad. How did couples do it when one parent moved four hours away and the other couldn't drive?

I prayed for an explanation that wouldn't leave Nathan feeling abandoned. "No, your dad lives too far away for that. You'll see him when he's in town."

I expected Nathan to start crying, and prepared to wrap my arms around him.

Instead, he let out a sigh. "*Phew!* I was just thinking that if I spent half the week with Dad, when I'm with him, I'd have to get up at three in the morning to get to school on time."

I kept my *phew* to myself. Leave it to my nine-going-on-thirty-five-year-old to do the math and decide that a four-hour commute wouldn't work for him.

Nathan went back to his homework. I turned my focus to my list. *Spaghetti noodles, tomato sauce, ground beef . . .*

Wait! Going-on-thirty-five-since-birth or not, Nathan is still a child. He should be upset.

Was he trying to shield my feelings? His world had unraveled. Just like I'd never expected to parent alone, Nathan surely never dreamed he'd end up like Jake and some of the boys on his baseball team.

"Hey, Nate, are you okay with not seeing your dad as often as other kids see theirs?"

"Yeah. I mean, I want to see him more. But I can't go to two different schools. Can I?"

"No." I sure hoped not!

The reality of what lay ahead for Nathan and Christian tore at my soul. No matter how often they saw their father, and regardless of how okay they seemed, my boys were getting hurt.

But as I watched Nathan take out his next worksheet, I recognized something: He really did seem fine at the moment. I sensed God's gentle protection over his heart. If working out the logistics of dividing his life between two homes gave Nathan peace, what a gift from God. We'd had plenty of teary moments since his dad left and we would have more. It would be hard enough when an official visitation plan ruled our schedule. For now, he was accepting a tough reality with maturity.

Divorce had hurled my sons into a world I had never experienced while growing up. No matter how hard I tried, I could not protect them from the pain, but God, being ever kind and faithful, knew exactly how to care for them.

———

The only thing more excruciating than seeing our world fall apart is watching our kids suffer in the wake of adult choices. Each day brings new questions, disappointments, and difficult conversations.

"Give me a sign of your goodness," David cried. How often do we need the same? Sometimes God answers by being kind to us. Other times His goodness comes through His care for those we love.

As you try to shield your children from what you wish could be different and find it impossible, know that God holds their hearts in ways you can't see. May you see a sign of His goodness to them today, even in the tears and tough answers.

Heavenly Father, it breaks my heart to see my children suffer. Be near me as I answer hard questions and deliver disappointing news. Help me remember that You love my kids more than I ever can and see the needs of their hearts. Amen.

TO TAKE INTO YOUR DAY

Read: Psalm 86

Consider: How has God cared for your children in ways that you couldn't?

Survival Tip: Ask a friend to join you in praying especially for your kids.

4

Is This a Joke?

*And we know that in all things God works
for the good of those who love him, who have been
called according to his purpose.*

Romans 8:28

"MAKE SURE YOUR ATTORNEY stresses that you're legally blind," friends reminded me.

"She will," I assured them. "If I milk that too much, though, it could backfire." I'd read an article about blind parents who'd lost custody of their kids because their ex-spouses presented them as unfit. This was not the time for a helpless act. Privately, as I counted the number of items on my to-do list that required finding transportation and wondered how long I could continue with work-from-home freelancing, I felt pretty unfit for the roles of breadwinner and Mom/Dad.

God, is this a joke? How can I manage a household if I

can't even drive? I'd already decided that Nathan would have to take the next season of Little League off.

I remembered my infamous kindergarten teacher, who couldn't grasp that I had a vision problem and not a learning problem. I'd been born with a rare genetic eye problem called achromatopsia, which causes complete color blindness, hypersensitivity to light, and vision that classified me legally blind. I'd heard numerous stories about that teacher telling Mom I must be dumb, eye doctors who insisted, "Stop treating your daughter like she's normal," and special education teachers who predicted sending me to a school for the blind. Had I shown them or what? I'd made it through public school and college; participated in drama, music, and public speaking; gotten married; maintained steady employment; and become a writer. I'd also become a mother. Now I was parenting alone. What would my kindergarten teacher have to say about that?

Those memories motivated the overcomer in me. What an opportunity to continue proving those naysayers wrong! Since when had low vision held me back from being a good mother? I'd become such a champion at adapting that my sons sometimes forgot I was visually impaired.

A new thought came to me: *If God allowed this, He must think I can do it.*

God brought to mind one of my favorite stories from

Scripture, when Jesus healed the man who'd been born blind: ". . . this happened so that the works of God might be displayed in him" (John 9:3), He told the disciples.

The work of God had been displayed through that man when Jesus healed him. Was it possible that He wanted to shine through my life in a different way?

As I reflected on my experience so far, I recognized that He was already in the process of doing that. He had sent me plenty of help through my church, friends, and family. He had created me to be a creative, resourceful woman who was not quick to give up. This season was not a joke at all, but a time for His work to be put on display, both for others and for me.

With His guidance I was capable of providing a secure home for my sons. Limited vision would simply force me to adapt in new ways, know when to ask for help, and rely more heavily on God.

Each of us has an area of weakness that forces us to rely on divine power. For me it's poor eyesight; for you it might be a health problem or something else. Our limitations can become convenient excuses for declaring, "I can't do this." They can cause others to see us as incapable of parenting alone. This is exactly when we need confidence that, in

God's power, we can do what is ahead of us. The challenge of single parenting will push our limits, but we also have a chance to let it nudge us out of our comfort zone and experience God doing the impossible.

The truth is that everyone has *something*. Some limitations are just more obvious. No matter what yours happen to be, ask God to empower you with strength, the resourcefulness to make things work, and the will to create the home your kids need.

God, help me recognize the unique strengths that You have equipped me with through my challenges. Replace my feelings of helplessness with determination to see Your power put on display, for others, for my children, and for me. Amen.

TO TAKE INTO YOUR DAY

Read: John 9:1–3

Consider: How might God's power be displayed through your life?

Survival Tip: List a few areas where you could seek help from friends or family.

5

Juggling Act

But those who hope in the LORD will renew their strength.
They will soar on wings like eagles; they will run
and not grow weary, they will walk and not be faint.

Isaiah 40:31

I HEADED TO THE KITCHEN and turned off the timer alerting me that the yeast was ready. Two years before my husband left, I'd started making as much as possible from scratch to save money. I didn't really have time to bake today between work and some dreaded phone calls, but we needed bread for lunches and kneading doubled as a stress release.

God, I feel completely overwhelmed.

I dumped in flour, olive oil, a little sugar and salt, and attacked the mass with a spoon.

The endless list of responsibilities sent my mind into a flurry of anxiety and resentment. How would I learn to balance it all?

I wasn't a stranger to juggling a job with household and parenting responsibilities that would normally be shared with a husband. For as long as we'd been married, my husband's income had required me to work as well. He usually worked weekends, so I'd tackled a lot of yard work and small projects alone or with the kids. A few years before, he'd had health problems that scared me into taking over paying the bills in case something happened to him. I hadn't minded doing whatever it took then. Why did it feel oppressive now? There was a huge difference between sometimes feeling like a single mom—as if I knew what that felt like—and actually being one.

Single moms do this much and more every day, I told myself. *Stop complaining.*

But when I thought about the daunting divorce process, the bills I couldn't pay, a house that was falling apart before my husband left, our pets, and keeping up with the daily tasks of being both Mom and Dad, it all felt like too much.

I don't want *to do everything!*

I sculpted the dough into two loaf shapes and prayed that it would rise.

The phone rang. It was my friend Susan. "You sound upset. What's up?"

I took a deep breath. "Oh, you know, just a lot to do. I took out my frustrations on bread dough."

"You're still baking bread?" She let out a sigh/laugh. "Why make extra work for yourself? Bread is cheap."

I sank onto the couch. "Maybe it's time to buy bread and bake the fun stuff."

"Sounds like a good plan. There's a bread outlet downtown. I'll take you next week."

She had a great point. What was I trying to prove? No wonder I couldn't keep up. God had the power to strengthen me through my fullest days, but it was pretty hard to soar on wings like eagles when I insisted on making life more difficult than it needed to be.

I focused what was left of my energy on the list of phone calls, all of which required me to tell one more banker or customer service agent why my financial situation was such a mess.

After that I would take a break and plot out how to make this new life of mine work without losing my sanity. What could I ask Christian to do? What could I ask Nathan to do? What needed to go (besides regular bread making)?

God, give me strength. Show me how to do this.

———

Life can be overwhelming enough when parents are working together, but when you're on your own it can feel impossible. You might be working outside the home for the very first time, or managing responsibilities that your husband took care of. Never mind the emotional toll of knowing life has changed.

As you call on God with your honest complaints and cries for superhuman strength, ask Him how you can also lighten the load. How can you stagger hard responsibilities, cut back on unnecessary things, and ask your kids for help? When parenting feels way too big for one person, take comfort in knowing you are doing it with a Father who promises to strengthen His weary children and be present for every task.

Lord, life was full before; now it is overloaded. This isn't going to end any time soon, and today I'm tired. Show me what to let go and what can't be avoided. Thank You for Your gentle ways of teaching me my limits. Amen.

TO TAKE INTO YOUR DAY

Read: Isaiah 40:28–31

Consider: What has becoming a single mom added to your list of responsibilities?

Survival Tip: This week come up with one unnecessary burden that you can eliminate.

6

Charity Case

All the believers were together and had everything
in common. They sold property and possessions
to give to anyone who had need.

Acts 2:44–45

THE EXCEL SPREADSHEET budget included every bill
for the month. Beside each item I'd written when the bill
was due and how it would be paid.

Cell phone: Me

Power: the church

I'd canceled cable, limited Netflix to live streaming, and
found a more affordable phone/Internet bundle. Once I'd
bought almost a week's worth of groceries with what some
spend on coffee. I could make just about anything from
scratch and lived simply. I still couldn't get around the fact
that, in addition to my parents helping me with legal fees,
Christian contributing financially, and Nathan having a

scholarship for school, I still needed the financial support my church had offered.

I've become a charity case. The thought plagued my already fragile ego. *I should be paying my own bills.*

I knew I was blessed to have a church that wanted to help, but I hated needing it. I took every writing and editing job that came my way, and I still couldn't stand on my own financially. What would happen when I started to pay rent?

Just be thankful, I ordered myself.

How often had I received anonymous cash and gift cards? I didn't consider those surprises charity, nor did I worry it was charity when a friend filled Nathan's entire school supply list.

I hadn't asked my church to pay these bills; they'd insisted.

"You give back in your own way," one of my friends had assured me.

I guess that's true. When the church collected school supplies for low-income families, it felt wonderful to pick up extra notebooks and pencil cases at the Dollar Store and add them to the collection box. When my friend Nancy asked me to watch her sons one afternoon a week and offered to pay me, I told her she didn't need to. Had I done that because I considered her a charity case? Of course not!

I wanted to watch Nancy's kids for free because she was my friend and I'd received so much generosity.

I repeatedly reminded myself of the passage in Acts where the early church had everything in common. If someone had a need, others in the church met it. They were even willing to sell property. I did not recall a verse implying that any of those on the receiving end were considered charity cases.

How dare I feel ashamed, for one second, over what others did out of kindness?

Someday I would be on the giving end. For now my job was to figure out how much income I needed to live on, be responsible with what I had, and thank God for every provision.

———

The realization that the loss of our husbands' income has forced us to need help from others only adds to the pain of seeing our dreams shattered. It's tempting to let this diminish our sense of worth, when actually it reflects how deeply people care about us.

Becoming a single mom might have put you in the position of accepting help that feels like charity. Whether it was offered or you had to ask, you probably feel like I did. Yet Scripture offers many examples that God wants His people to help those in need, going so far as to call it more blessed to give than to receive. Ask God to fill you with the humility to receive with thanksgiving and show you how you contribute in ways that can't be measured by a dollar amount.

God, thank You for providing for me and my children. Forgive the pride that clouds my gratitude. Remind me what a joy it is to give. Provide opportunities for me to help others. But most of all, make me more thankful. Amen.

TO TAKE INTO YOUR DAY

Read: Acts 2:42–47

Consider: How is God providing for you through your church, family, or friends?

Survival Tip: When we have received a lot, it feels good to give. This week do something kind for someone else. Hint: It doesn't have to require a lot of money or time. Send an encouraging card to another single mom, help a friend with a project, contribute to a food drive . . .

7

Single Again

For your Maker is your husband—the LORD Almighty is
his name—the Holy One of Israel is your Redeemer;
he is called the God of all the earth.

Isaiah 54:5

"HOW MANY OF YOU are married?" the pastor asked.
"Raise your hands."

My hand instinctively started to go up before I realized
my mistake.

"How many of you are single?"

I kept my hand in my lap. I didn't fall into that category either. Technically, I was still a married woman. Soon
I would be single. Suddenly that felt very strange.

I had been married for over half my life.

My husband and I started dating soon after my twen-
tieth birthday. Eleven months later, he asked me to marry

him. When I walked down the aisle in my princess-like white dress, I expected to be married forever.

I looked at my left hand, where I now wore an emerald ring. I'd taken off my wedding ring after my first consultation with an attorney, tossing it into my purse as a friend helplessly looked on. Before Nathan came home from school and Christian returned from work, I'd slipped on the emerald and hoped they wouldn't notice.

As the pastor continued with his point, I had a flashback to my days in the church college group when we had regular discussions about singleness.

Singleness. That awful word. We were encouraged to be content with singleness. Funny that none of us required special encouragement to be content with having a boyfriend or fiancé.

What would I do once a judge's signature declared me single again?

Learn to be content, I guessed. Try not to dwell on the reality that, for me, *single* was not my choice.

The pastor's sermon became white noise in the background of my thoughts. I was no longer a wife. I would never have a twenty-fifth wedding anniversary. I would not grow old with the man I married at twenty-one.

The man in front of me wrapped his arm around his wife. Would I ever feel that again?

I felt God's presence envelop me. *There are benefits in being single.*

True. I could make my own decisions, enjoy girlfriend time, make deviled eggs without him complaining about the smell. But right now none of that made up for the lack of companionship and a broken family.

There are other benefits; deeper ones. I thought about that.

When had I ever enjoyed a life of just God and me? When had I truly let Him be the love of my life and meet the needs of my heart? Not during the years between my first high school date and marrying my husband. I'd been one of those girls who thought she needed a boyfriend in order to feel valuable. Now that I didn't have a man in my life and my heart ached with the pain of rejection, I needed Him more than ever.

My desire changed from a willingness to be content being single to hope that I would make the most of this time. I still didn't want singleness, but if God could bring something lovely out it, like a deeper relationship with Him, then I could be content with that.

***

Regardless of what ended your *married* status, the reality of *I'm single again* probably stirs a flood of "I will never have . . ." grief. What are you supposed to do with your wedding ring?

How will you face your anniversary and those places that became special because they were *your* special places? How can the benefits possibly be worth the losses and loneliness?

Today, lean into the arms of the One who meant it when He said, "For your Maker is your husband" (Isaiah 54:5). Ask Him to meet the deep needs that no human husband can understand, let alone meet. As you make sense of what's lost, draw closer to the Father, who can bring beautiful things out of the rubble, including a deeper trust in Him and contentment in His plan for you.

Heavenly Father, I didn't plan to ever be single again. Comfort me as I learn to accept what I don't want. Show me benefits to this new life. Help me live it well as You draw me closer. Show me what a perfect Husband You are. Amen.

TO TAKE INTO YOUR DAY

Read: Isaiah 54:4–6
Consider: What are some benefits of being single?
Survival Tip: Schedule extra time with God into your day, just to get to know Him more.

8

Not an Option

But he said to me, "My grace is sufficient for you,
for my power is made perfect in weakness."'
Therefore I will boast all the more gladly about
my weaknesses, so that Christ's power may rest on me.

2 Corinthians 12:9

I RAN MY FINGERTIPS over my wrist.

Why hasn't she replied?

Earlier that week I'd poured out my frustrations to a friend in an e-mail. How could she have read that and not written back?

I shouldn't have sent that whiny message. When will I stop being so needy?

Compared to divorce, a delayed reply should have rolled over me like a breeze. But these days every slight was magnified times fifty. Instead of moving on with my day, I'd let it drive me to an old temptation.

Depression had been my thorn in the flesh since college, sometimes triggering self-injury, dark thoughts, and relapses of anorexic tendencies. I hadn't been seriously depressed in several years, but on this lonely morning when I was disappointed in a friend and myself and had bigger problems to deal with than an unanswered e-mail, releasing emotional pain through physical pain felt like the solution.

I almost gave in. Then I yanked my hands apart. *Stop it! What are you thinking?*

Your sons need you to be strong. You are all they have right now. Someone needs to be the grown-up and hold it together. Sinking into the pit is not an option anymore.

Didn't I have a right to be depressed? Wouldn't it be expected? I was losing my marriage! My sons no longer had their dad around.

It's okay to be devastated. But you are not allowed to cry out in self-destructive ways.

Tears welled up.

You've come too far to cave now.

Did I want this crisis to send me backward?

I wanted to be an example of resilience, not a woman who gave in to despair even if I had a right to. I would not let someone else's choice do that to me.

Lord, help me. If anything has the power to send me spiraling, divorce and learning to survive as a single parent does.

Or maybe this journey would be my ultimate test.

Maybe this was my opportunity to let my heavenly Father's sufficiency bring out hidden strengths. Yes, depression had gripped me in the past. Yes, I was vulnerable right now, but God promised to make His power perfect in weakness.

I had plenty of friends to call on in moments of distress, including the one I knew would reply eventually. My church had a counseling ministry if I needed it. I had a loving God who was available to me constantly. Instead of choosing a harmful path, I would make up my mind each day to call on His grace and strength.

If anyone has a valid excuse to be depressed, a single mom does. Perhaps you have already found yourself fighting depression or other temptations.

"But he said to me, 'My grace is sufficient for you, for my power is made perfect in weakness.' Therefore I will boast all the more gladly about my weaknesses, so that Christ's power may rest on me" (2 Corinthians 12:9).

When we feel the pull of the pit, we have access to the One who makes it possible to fight it. In His strength, sometimes combined with outside resources, we can make up our mind to see this journey through with perseverance that leaves people wondering what our secret is.

Today, no matter how hard things get, hold on to the thought that it is completely okay to feel needy, to cry, and even to whine about the unfairness of it all. It is okay to need therapy, a support group, medication, or all of the above. But what is God telling you it is not okay to do? How has He already made His grace sufficient for you?

Heavenly Father, others are depending on me. Be my strength today, and tomorrow, and every day. Help me feel Your love. Send friends when I need them and more of Your presence when they can't be reached. Thank You for all You will do in me through this. Amen.

TO TAKE INTO YOUR DAY

Read: 2 Corinthians 12:7–10

Consider: What unhealthy patterns are you vulnerable to? What do you need to decide is not an option for you?

Survival Tip: Make a list of friends you can call when you are depressed or tempted to give in to destructive temptations?

SECTION 2

surviving
survival mode

9

So Tired

"Blessed are those who mourn, for they will be comforted."
Matthew 5:4

ONE OF MY FAVORITE NIGHTS of the week had come and I didn't have the energy to enjoy it. My fellow choir members practiced the song for the upcoming Sunday morning while I could barely get the words out. What had happened to my voice? Every line came out sounding breathy. I didn't bother with the high notes. After over twenty years of singing, this was the best I could do? Through all the turmoil, singing continued to be a source of joy, an outlet for emotions, a break from the divorce process and load of responsibility. My pastors encouraged me to continue with worship team and choir. Now all I could do was force out whispers and try to sit up straight.

"You are such a reflection of God's grace," women at

church had told me. "You are handling this with amazing strength." So much for grace and strength tonight.

I took off my reading glasses, let my shoulders slump, and gave up on the song. My mind swam with the week's stresses:

A mountain of forms for government services that I'd been encouraged to apply for but didn't want any part of.

Bills in my husband's name that were still coming to me.

Another overdue notice from the mortgage company.

Where would the boys and I live once the house foreclosed?

Should I keep waiting on my attorney to return that message I left or risk being an annoying client and call again?

Choir ended with me choking on tears through the closing prayer.

"Hey, you." My friend Jill wrapped her arm around me. "How are you doing?"

My lip trembled. Jill squeezed my shoulder. Tears dripped. "I'm just … tired."

She pulled me closer.

"And now I can't even sing."

"Oh, Jeanette." Jill's tight voice gave away that she was ready to cry too.

I poured out the contents of my worn-out brain.

On the other side of me, Anita took my hand. Margo came over to listen. The rest of the choir members were kind enough to trickle out without drawing more attention to me. After I finished sharing the source of my tears, Jill pulled me into a hug and my friends took turns praying.

Nathan walked into the choir room from Bible club before we said amen. When I finally composed myself for our ride home, I experienced the relief that comes from giving up the tough act. Three sisters in Christ now knew I'd officially run out of steam.

I didn't want to make a regular habit of choir meltdowns, but on this night I thanked God for allowing one. I'd received comfort, prayer, and a few suggestions for how I might lighten my stress load. God would use Jill, Margo, and Anita to support me in ways that I knew grew out of this moment when I was too tired to be a picture of God's grace.

Sometimes the best thing we can do is let someone see what a mess we feel like. When we allow ourselves to stop acting so capable, God has a way of providing exactly what we need but are afraid to ask for. Through supportive friends we find someone to cry or pray with, a listening ear, and even sources of practical help. But receiving these things requires us to admit we're at the end of our rope, both to God and to those He provides.

Why do we think reflecting God's grace requires stuffing

all signs of emotional need, when Jesus wept on many occasions and told a crowd, "Blessed are those who mourn . . ." (Matthew 5:4)? The Psalms are full of laments from a needy heart. How much more permission do we need to let caring friends in so they know how to help?

Lord, I feel like David, poor and needy. I want so badly to handle this crisis with grace, but my strength drains away with every added concern. Today, I just want someone to wrap comforting arms around me. Meet the needs of my heart today. Amen.

TO TAKE INTO YOUR DAY

Read: Psalm 86

Consider: What is wearing you out right now? What would help you most? Be honest.

Survival Tip: Spend some time pouring out your need to God. Ask Him to send the support you need today.

~ 10 ~

"Why Were You Crying?"

[There is] a time to weep and a time to laugh,
a time to mourn and a time to dance.

Ecclesiastes 3:4

NATHAN DIDN'T TAKE HIS EYES off me as he got under the covers. I reached for the book we'd been enjoying at bedtime and attempted to hide my red, puffy eyes behind my reading glasses.

"Mom?" His voice brimmed with concern. I knew what was coming next. "Why were you crying?"

I looked at his face, those expressive brown eyes that did me in every time. I relived the moment when Nathan walked in on me crying with Jill, Anita, and Margo as they prayed for me after choir practice. How upsetting that must have been for him!

I stroked his hair. "Oh, I was just having a hard night. I'm better now."

"Really?"

"Yes. Really." I read a couple of pages, then we said his prayers. I kissed him good night.

Nathan gave me a long hug. I sat on his bunk until he fell asleep, feeling like the weakest mom alive.

I've probably scarred him for life. That time with my friends was so helpful, but I need to learn to save my emotions for when there isn't a chance of Nathan being present. Things are hard enough for him without also seeing his mom crying in public.

The scene after choir practice replayed in my mind again, this time from a different perspective. I saw Nathan standing back, observing the emotional moment. He had seen me crying, but he had also watched three kind women support and pray for his mom.

"You need to let your sons see your pain," friends had told me repeatedly. "It's okay for them to know this is hard on you."

He had definitely seen that. And he had witnessed God's people at their best, praying, comforting, and acting Christlike.

How could I expect Christian and Nathan to be honest with me about their emotions over their dad leaving if they never saw me shed a tear? How could I expect them to understand how difficult it was to go through a divorce, keep up with added responsibilities, and face an uncertain future if I went through each stress and loss with stoic resolve? They needed to see that I'd loved their dad enough to cry when our marriage fell apart, and that it hurt to be on our own, know we would lose the house, and rely on others for survival. I didn't want to cross the line into burdening my sons with every tear, but maybe it would benefit them to learn that remaining strong and stable through difficult times did not require stuffing tears, and that it helped to let some of the pressure out once in a while.

"Who understands tears more than a child?" someone had once asked me. Nathan's tenderness at bedtime revealed that he did. He just wanted to know what caused them.

There is "a time to weep" (Ecclesiastes 3:4). Kids often understand this better than we do.

What a beautiful gift God gave us by creating us with a deep well of emotions and filling His Word with passages and stories that make room for every one of them. So why do we feel the need to keep our sadness hidden when it makes the most sense to express it? Why is it that we'll cry in front of our kids over a misplaced cell phone but fear that they'll be ruined forever if they see us weep after a blow that changed everything?

As you encourage your children to express their feelings, remember that they really will be okay if they also see more of yours. Today, ask God to help you recognize when you need to toughen up for your kids' sake, and when it's time to let them share your tears.

Father, I want to be strong for my children, but not so strong that they think I'm completely unaffected by this. Thank You for being a God who allowed Yourself to weep when tears were called for. Help me as I let my kids see that I feel them too. Amen.

TO TAKE INTO YOUR DAY

Read: Ecclesiastes 3:1–8

Consider: When was the last time your kids saw you cry?

Survival Tip: Let your kids see your pain now and then.

11

Not a Burden

Do not withhold good from those to whom it is due,
when it is in your power to act.

Proverbs 3:27

"YOU AND NATHAN walked to the store at night?"

"We were completely out of toilet paper and Christian was at work," I explained to Susan. "It didn't get dark until the walk home."

Susan playfully swatted me. "I would have driven you, or brought you some TP."

I shrugged. "I didn't want to—"

"Be a bother? Don't be silly. You are not a burden! Next time call, okay?"

None of my friends treated me like a burden. Yet I couldn't shake the fear of becoming one. It didn't matter how many times I heard, "This is how God's family is supposed to work." I still feared the day when someone would get sick of carting me around, or I'd be seen as taking advantage.

While tidying my nightstand I spotted a piece of notebook paper that I'd brought home from Bible study months earlier. My mind replayed a scene from the morning after my husband moved out for the temporary separation that became permanent. I could still hear the sniffles and heartfelt prayers of my small group. During the discussion, the ladies circulated a notebook. By the time it came around to me, every woman in the room had written down her name and phone number to call if I needed a ride, to talk, or anything else. Since then that list had grown . . . and grown.

I had friends who especially enjoyed taking me shopping. They said they looked forward to it because it gave us an excuse to hang out. Sherry cut my hair at no charge. Choir members made sure I didn't walk to or from church in the dark or the rain, and Nathan always had a ride to school in bad weather. If spiders overtook the house or something needed fixing that was beyond Christian, I knew whom to call. I hadn't gone on a frantic search for any of this assistance; it came to me. Through these resources I'd gained new friends and seen relationships deepen.

It was time to let go of my fear of being a burden and see it all as a blessing. As I'd heard so many times, my friends were doing exactly what God had asked them to do.

As a low-vision student I'd been taught to do as much as possible on my own but also have the smarts to know when to ask for help. I thought I knew how to do that. This being-on-my-own thing was taking learning to ask for help to a whole new level.

The truth was I couldn't handle everything on my own. Transportation was a legitimate need. Some things, like walking alone at night in a less-than-ideal neighborhood, were just plain unsafe. One day God would reward my precious village of support. For now, He wanted me to make use of their kindness.

Limitation or not, asking for help is hard, especially when we know we will be in need of it for a long time. In a society where we are molded to be independent and achieve as much as possible on our own, it's easy to forget that God created us to thrive in community. We need our community more than ever as single moms.

Proverbs 3:27 says, "Do not withhold good from those to whom it is due, when it is in your power to act." What a delight it is to have friends and family members who live this out! If you are struggling with fear of being a bother, consider what it might feel like to want desperately to give someone a hand that she refuses to take. Ask God for the humility to recognize your limits and to gratefully make use of the friends He is using to tell you, "You don't need to do this by yourself."

Lord, thank You for placing me in a community filled with resources. Forgive me for times when I insisted on doing it all by myself. Show me when it's best to tackle a project alone and when it would be wiser to call for help. Send the extra hand I need today. Amen.

TO TAKE INTO YOUR DAY

Read: Matthew 25:31–40
Consider: When have you struggled unnecessarily because you refused to ask for help?
Survival Tip: Take someone up on her offer to help you.

12

Wallow Days

*The LORD is close to the brokenhearted
and saves those who are crushed in spirit.*

Psalm 34:18

I STARED AT MY MONITOR, struggling to focus on an editing job. Most days my need for income motivated me to stay on task. Today, all I wanted to do was mope.

I'd heard of women spending whole days in bed. How was that possible? How would Nathan get breakfast and off to school if I stayed under the covers? I had work to do, bill collectors to call, government-subsidized housing options to consider. Besides, a mother with a history of depression couldn't afford to flirt with despair.

I threw myself back into work. My mind refused to stay engaged. I reread the same paragraph three times, cut a sentence then pasted it back in, added a comma that may or may not have been needed. *This project isn't even a good fit for me*, I grumbled to myself. *I hate being so desperate.* My throat ached.

I pulled up my e-mail. Maybe it would help to ask a few friends to pray for me.

Please say a prayer. I'm having a hard morning . . .

Moments later, I found a reply from Margo.

I'm sorry, sweetheart. There is no getting around it. Divorce stinks.

Yes, it did.

You're entitled to an occasional wallow day.

Was I?

Her message felt like an invitation. Was it possible that giving in to one sulky day might prevent an emotional crash later?

I thanked Margo, saved my work, closed it, and started mindlessly browsing blogs while deciding which friend to call and wallow with.

Or was I not supposed to do that? How did God want me to spend a wallow day?

"The LORD is close to the brokenhearted . . ." Psalm 34:18 had become one of my favorite verses. Maybe today was about experiencing it firsthand.

Awareness that God wanted me to wallow with Him drew me out of my chair and into my bedroom.

I pulled out my journal and wrote a long prayer, pouring out all that kept me from focusing on work. I took a walk without bothering to put on makeup, and then a nap. Tatiana, my favorite of our two cats, snuggled against me and purred.

I pictured Jesus sitting beside me too, His hand on my back as I rested, ready to gather me up if I needed Him to. An hour later, I got up and baked banana bread so Nathan and Christian would come home to a treat to distract them from my bloodshot eyes. By the time I walked to the school to pick up Nathan, my spirit felt less heavy.

That was the first of several occasional wallow days. I knew I was due for one when I couldn't think and everything made me tear up. I found that when I gave myself permission to drag my way through mindless activity, the entire time calling on God for what I needed to make the next day better, I was twice as productive later. But more than that, these days connected me with my Source of comfort.

Who wouldn't want to drag around when life is this overwhelming? You don't have time to mope, but you want to and sometimes need to in order to face the next step.

"The LORD is close to the brokenhearted and saves those who are crushed in spirit" (Psalm 34:18). We experience God's closeness in a unique way when we give our spirits time to droop for a while. Whether you are having a weekend when you don't want to get out of bed or choose to work from home so you don't have to hide your tears, walk through sadness with the One who knows your need. Ask God to stay close as, even for one hour, you give in to emotions, stop pushing through, and let your day reflect how you feel inside.

Heavenly Father, thank You for being close to brokenhearted women like me. Let me feel Your presence today. Help me know how to spend days when I just want to curl up and complain to You. Thank You for giving me the freedom to, and for using these times to strengthen me. Amen.

TO TAKE INTO YOUR DAY

Read: Psalm 42

Consider: When have you benefited from giving in to a difficult day?

Survival Tip: Give yourself room to have an occasional wallow day. How will you connect with God for comfort?

13

More Than We Need

And my God will meet all your needs according
to the riches of his glory in Christ Jesus.

Philippians 4:19

"WE HAVE A SURPRISE for you," Julie said after our evening Bible study wrapped up and we were gathering our kids.

Kim pointed toward a box. "That's for you. Everyone brought some groceries and household items tonight. We just wanted to do something for you and the boys."

My prideful side wanted to feel ashamed or offended, but by now I knew better. These couples loved us and wanted to be kind, so I hugged Julie and Kim and thanked God for sending me groceries just when I was preparing to make a list.

Once we got home, Julie's husband had Christian help him haul in two giant boxes filled with canned and packaged goods, treats for Nathan's lunches, paper towels, toilet paper, new toothbrushes, scented hand soap, and cleaning products.

"Nutella!" Nathan held up the squatty jar and grinned. "I've always wanted to try this."

Every time we opened that nutty chocolate and spread it on Saltines (at a friend's granddaughter's suggestion), my heart melted with gratitude for God's way of supplying beyond what we needed to survive. "And my God will meet all your needs according to the riches of his glory in Christ" (Philippians 4:19) became evident every time I made a shopping list and remembered items that I didn't need because we still had some of our stash from the Bible study group. It became true again when I had lunch with a friend before a trip to the store and she slipped a card with a twenty-dollar bill inside across the table. "I wanted to buy some of your groceries today," or when another friend surprised me with a fifty-dollar trip to Trader Joe's. I understood why Paul called the generosity he received "a fragrant offering." Each gift became just that for us. Paychecks that arrived in time for me to fill our refrigerator myself started feeling like gifts too.

After my husband left, I kept waiting to start living on Ramen noodles and homemade pinto beans and to send Nathan off to school with skimpy lunches. That day never came. We did eat Ramen noodles because they were cheap,

I had a growing boy and a young adult in the house, and the boys liked them. I made those pinto beans often because burritos were a favorite fallback meal. My parents cringed when they heard how far I stretched my grocery budget, fearing that we weren't eating enough, but our cupboards, the contents of the Crock-Pot, Nathan's rosy cheeks, and Christian's thick curls proved that we never went hungry. In moments when I worried, *Is it okay for my sons to know friends bought our groceries sometimes?* I asked God to engrave this time in their memories as inspiration to someday help someone else get what they needed, plus more.

When we are raising growing children alone, fear of seeing them go without a meal or not have all of their nutritional needs met plagues us. Hopefully you have seen God provide in ways that surprised you—gifts that you know must have gone up like fragrant offerings to Him because that's what they were to you. Maybe they came through cash slipped into your hand, a bag of groceries dropped off at your door, or a friend who said, "When I went through a hard time you helped me; now I want to help you."

The sad truth is that you have probably had to cut back in many ways. Going out for dinner might be a thing of the past or a rare treat. Yet God promises to supply our needs, so how is He doing that for you? If you are experiencing a day when you have no idea how you will buy milk, let alone after-school snacks, ask Him to bring Philippians 4:19 and His other promises to provide to life for you. How has His track record so far given you hope?

Father, You are such a faithful Provider. Thank You for the many ways You have surpassed my prayers by going beyond what my children and I need to survive. Reward the kindness of my generous friends. Let this time motivate me to contribute to needs when I am able. Amen.

TO TAKE INTO YOUR DAY

Read: Philippians 4:14–20

Consider: How is God providing for your basic needs? When has He sent more than you needed?

Survival Tip: Write this verse on a 3 x 5 card or in your journal: "I was young and now I am old, yet I have never seen the righteous forsaken or their children begging bread" (Psalm 37:25). Put it somewhere where you will see it often.

14

A Big Dog with a Big Bark

Be merciful to me, Lord, for I am in distress;
my eyes grow weak with sorrow,
my soul and body with grief.

Psalm 31:9

I'D HEARD ABOUT KIDS acting out when their parents went through a divorce, but dogs?

Christian, Nathan, and I chased our hyperactive pit bull/lab mix, Belle, down the street for the third time in two weeks. What was her problem? Was she looking for her master? Did she not like change?

Christian grabbed her by the collar. She wiggled free. A neighbor caught Belle long enough for me to wrap my arms around her middle and lug our fifty-pound escapee home. I wanted to give her to Christian to carry but feared we might drop her in the handoff.

"That's it." I caught my breath. "She needs to go."

"Good riddance," Christian mumbled. Even my quiet oldest son had had it with Belle.

"No!" Nathan burst into tears.

"We can't let her keep doing this." Neighbors had called Animal Control twice because Belle got out while we were gone. We didn't have any warnings left and couldn't afford a fine.

Friends had been urging me to surrender Belle. We had no idea how long the mortgage company would allow us to stay in the house, and pets, especially a dog, would complicate my search for an affordable rental. I had to consider our budget. If it was between buying pet food or people food, Christian and Nathan came before Belle and the cats.

This final escape sealed Belle's future. Two weeks later, a friend helped me pack Belle into her crate and deliver her to the Humane Society. I felt like a Dickens-era mother who'd just handed over her child to the workhouse.

God, this isn't fair.

The only family members who didn't grieve Belle's departure were the cats.

A cloud of silent distress hung in our home. Belle might not have been the smartest dog on the block, but she was family. Until we gave her up, I didn't appreciate the sense of protection her presence provided. Though she probably wouldn't have done anything but lick an intruder into submission, she was still a big dog with a big bark. We'd loved Belle in all her lunacy, inability to pass obedience school, refusal to stay off the furniture, and annoying escapes. Now she was gone, not because she got old and passed away, but because circumstances forced us to surrender her to strangers.

Tatiana and Princess fought for the throne of our household, oblivious to the fact that we would part with them eventually too. I comforted Nathan while silently resenting the cruel reality that Belle represented what we needed to start getting used to—loss.

Being a single mom means facing countless painful losses, including letting go of pets. Parting with something we love might be the practical thing to do, but it still rips us apart. Our friends can help us with the job, but we are the ones who must break the news to our kids, hear them cry, and feel the absence, knowing more sad good-byes are coming.

If you haven't had to let go of a pet, you may have parted with other precious things, like heirlooms or your house. Maybe moving forced your kids to give up a favorite activity or leave friends behind. It's possible you've lost so much that you stopped keeping track. All you know is that pieces of your life keep slipping away.

As you cry out to God and seek Him for how to comfort

your children, know that He cares about all our griefs, even our tears over pets and material things. If it's important to us, it's important to Him. Give yourself a moment today to express your sadness to your loving Father, who grieves along with you. Ask Him for a glimpse of the good things He has waiting for you and your children in the future.

Father, my losses may not have been deaths, but they feel just as final. Comfort me and my kids as we let go of things we love. Let me see You fill the holes with new things that could only come from You. Amen.

TO TAKE INTO YOUR DAY

Read: Psalm 31:19–24

Consider: Which losses have been the most painful?

Survival Tip: Take time to talk to your kids about something they've had to let go of that was precious to them.

15

Girls' Night Out at Costco

Two are better than one, because they have
a good return for their labor.

Ecclesiastes 4:9

I TOUCHED UP MY LIP GLOSS and pulled on my favorite boots. The doorbell rang. I grabbed my purse.

"Christian, Nancy's here. Call my cell if you need anything."

"Can you get more of those fish sticks?" Christian called from the kitchen.

I followed Nancy to her van. It was time for Girls' Night Out . . . at Costco.

Nancy and I met at our kids' school. We grew closer when we found ourselves going through divorces at the same time, and Nancy hired me to update her résumé.

When she needed someone to watch her sons one afternoon a week, I couldn't bring myself to accept payment from a fellow struggling single mom, so she said thank you by occasionally watching Nathan or showing up with pizza so I wouldn't have to cook dinner. Nancy was the one who thought up the Costco routine. "We can split bulk packages of meat and paper products."

The chance to save money became an eagerly awaited outing that allowed us to get out of the house, talk, and catch up with each other. Until shared pain drew Nancy and me together, the only things we had in common were school, church, and the age of our youngest sons. Now that we were both learning to survive on one income and navigate what felt like a never-ending divorce process, we had a special connection.

One Friday a month, Nancy picked me up after work and Christian watched the kids. Over $1.50 Costco hot dog combos we compared lists and coupons. If we didn't have time for dinner, we munched on samples while we shopped. I introduced her to my favorite tuna and she sold me on the raviolis her boys loved. We exchanged secrets for making ground beef and chicken more interesting. What we didn't need in bulk, we picked up at a regular grocery store before heading home.

During one pre-shopping meal Nancy started laughing. "I guess this is our version of Girls' Night Out."

"Yeah, some women go to clubs on Friday nights; we head to the food court." I crumpled my hot dog wrapper and reached for my list. "We should post this on Facebook. Our friends will be totally jealous."

Just for fun I did post it later. Within minutes I got comments from envious moms.

Invite me next time!

We found that "two are better than one" applied even to shopping for tuna and paper towels. Nancy provided the transportation; I provided the babysitter. Between shopping trips we supported each other with prayer, willingness to listen, and empathy. We were bonded to each other as newly single moms and sisters in the One who was keeping our lives from crumbling to pieces.

Adjusting to life as a single mom can be lonely and tedious. While our couple-friends have date nights, we sit at home and wonder how we'll afford laundry soap and who will watch the kids for that one hour on Monday afternoons when their dad used to be home for them. This is when friendship built on mutual support feels like a gift from above.

God has beautiful methods for bringing friends into our lives who allow us to experience the power in "two are better than one" (Ecclesiastes 4:9). By connecting with other single moms, we can share burdens, exchange ideas, and even find creative ways of having a social life. If you are feeling isolated and overwhelmed, ask God to send another single mom into your life, not only for your own benefit, but for hers as well.

Lord, thank You for my friends, especially those who are eager to make this life a bit easier. Thank You for showing me that two really are better than one, especially when the bond is held by You. Send me an opportunity to share a burden with another overloaded mom. Thank You in advance for what You will do through this friendship. Amen.

TO TAKE INTO YOUR DAY

Read: Ecclesiastes 4:9–12

Consider: How have you been helped by connecting with other single moms?

Survival Tip: Call another overwhelmed mom and brainstorm some ways that you can support each other.

⌒ 16 ⌒

Buses and White Canes

"Have I not commanded you? Be strong and courageous.
Do not be afraid; do not be discouraged, for the LORD your
God will be with you wherever you go."

Joshua 1:9

FORREST SAT AT MY DINING ROOM table taking notes. I'd sung with him in choir for years. As of today he was my mobility instructor through Services for the Blind and Visually Impaired, assigned to teach me the public transportation system. If I was going to survive as a non-driving single mom, I needed to brave the bus. Knowing my friends, they wouldn't let me take it often, but I couldn't expect them to be my taxi service forever. Their kindness had strengthened me to explore other resources. Already Services for the Blind had provided me with tools for making everyday life easier. They were ordering a computer with a large screen so I could be more productive in my work.

Only one thing hindered me from fully embracing the adventure of mobility training.

"Have you ever used a white cane?"

"No." My response came out like, *Why would I need one of those?*

None of the special teachers I'd worked with between fourth and ninth grade had suggested a cane. According to Forrest, riding the city bus with a reduced-fare disabled pass and crossing intersections alone called for learning the skill.

"It's for identification more than anything else," he assured me. "It tells drivers, 'This woman probably can't see you.'"

I struggled over the idea of traveling with a universal symbol of blindness after decades of learning to navigate the world without appearing disabled. Wasn't I going through enough of an identity crisis?

The first time I attempted a solo bus trip without using that awkward white stick, I understood why Forrest highly recommended one. In the years since I last took public transportation, I'd forgotten how utterly petrifying it felt to learn my way around town with limited eyesight. As Forrest predicted, bus drivers were more willing to help a person identified as disabled than they were a woman who appeared perfectly capable until she asked him to announce when he arrived at her stop. This no longer felt like an adventurous step of independence, but more like being thrown into a hostile foreign land. Maybe it would be better to keep calling friends for rides.

Instead, I set up my next lesson with Forrest and asked God to give me the courage to brave not only the bus but also that dreaded white cane. With every bus trip God boosted my confidence and hope that I could make it as a mom who couldn't drive. Once I finished my training, I could decide for myself whether I truly needed a white cane.

"Be strong and courageous," verse 9 from Joshua 1 reminded me. I thanked God that, though taking the bus and labeling myself *blind* was far less dramatic than His people entering the promised land, He would be with me through every step.

Once we have accepted our new life, our imaginations open up to new possibilities, some of which require giant leaps out of our comfort zones. Suddenly we understand why, before Joshua led the Israelites across the Jordan River, God felt the need to repeat, "Be strong and courageous."

Being a single parent might not require you to learn the public bus system, but you've probably had to do other things that called for courage. Perhaps you are considering going back to school or applying for a more challenging position at work that pays better but involves learning new skills. Whichever door God is opening, you are probably excited but scared. You might even be tempted to forget the whole thing. Times like this remind us why we need to be *told* to have courage. What a relief it is to know that when God says, "Be strong and courageous" (Joshua 1:9), He also promises to be with us as we go forward, afraid or not.

Heavenly Father, I don't want to be stuck where I am forever, but improving my life means doing some scary things. Help me in those moments when I'm tempted to hold myself back. Show me the rewards of being courageous. Amen.

TO TAKE INTO YOUR DAY

Read: Joshua 1:1–9

Consider: What new challenges are you considering right now?

Survival Tip: Look up a few famous quotes about courage. Write out your favorite and keep it in a place where you'll see it often.

SECTION 3

preventing an emotional wreck

17

"What about Us?"

Don't look out only for your own interests,
but take an interest in others, too.

Philippians 2:4 *NLT*

"WHY ARE YOU SO GRUMPY?" The tension in Nathan's voice told me he was ready to lose it. It didn't seem to bother him that we were walking down a street where we regularly encountered people we knew.

"Why do you think?" I snapped without meaning to. "Things are stressful right now. I'm tired."

Maybe I'd picked the wrong afternoon for a trip to Walmart. A difficult day had left me testy and incapable of dealing with a sulky fourth grader. What was his problem? There were worse hardships than walking a few blocks to buy the shoes he desperately needed. Christian had been in a bad mood all week too. Did they have any idea what it was like to be me right now? I wanted to stop Nathan on the sidewalk and spill every reason why I might possibly be grumpy. We were already making a scene; why not go for an Oscar-caliber performance? Instead, Nathan's words stopped *me.*

"What about us?" His voice cracked. His lip and chin quivered.

That question hit me square in the heart. The next thing I knew I was fighting back tears too. What a pathetic mother/son pair we must have made. I wrapped my arm around Nathan's shoulders. What *about* him and Christian? I guess I'd assumed that since they acted fine, God was sparing them. In all the times I'd been encouraged to let my sons see my pain, acknowledging or even checking in on theirs had never come up. Did I expect them to stay okay forever? Their dad had been gone for several months. The holidays were approaching, and they would be very different this year. As I watched Nathan swat at tears, I saw him as a child who had lost just as much as I had; his losses were just different. If I'd been in Nathan's place, would I have had a clue what my mom was going through? I hope I would have been half as sensitive as he was, but at some point I would have cried, "What about me?" too.

"Nate, I'm sorry." I searched through my purse for a tissue. "It is completely okay for you to be upset."

"Why did Dad have to leave, anyway?"

"I don't know." That seemed like the only appropriate

answer, because at that moment none of this made sense. But Nathan's tears sure did. The same went for Christian's moodiness.

God, forgive me. I've been selfish. We stopped so I could give him a hug. Now that I'd learned to let my kids see my pain, it was time to see theirs. Christian and Nathan had very different temperaments and were at different stages of life, but they had one thing in common—they were hurting whether they said so or not.

It's hard to admit, but when our kids seem to be sailing through the storm, it takes a lot of pressure off. We don't have to feel guilty or helpless or set our own emotions aside long enough to share theirs. We get to say, "My child is doing really well" and leave everyone marveling over our well-adjusted children. But when we consider how many tears we've shed and how much our children have endured, why does it surprise us when they suddenly get grouchy or teary or even angry?

"Don't look out only for your own interests, but take an interest in others, too" (Philippians 2:4 NLT). God often uses outbursts of emotions to remind us that our children have a lot more going on inside than they let on sometimes. Will we brush aside their feelings or take an interest in them? No matter how we've responded in the past, we can pray that from this day on we will be willing to sit with them in the ash heap like Job's friends did—or like our kids have already done for us on occasion.

Lord, forgive me for times when my own pain blinded me to what my kids were going through. Help me be more sensitive. Show me when I need to believe the words, "I'm fine," and when I need to find out how they are really doing. Amen.

TO TAKE INTO YOUR DAY

Read: Job 2:11–13

Consider: When was the last time you saw your kids cry over all that has happened? How did you handle it?

Survival Tip: Take some time to ask your children how they are doing.

18

Just Enough Truth

For the LORD gives wisdom; from his mouth
come knowledge and understanding.

Proverbs 2:6

JUST WHEN I THOUGHT Nathan had calmed down
from his teary moment on the way to Walmart, more came
out. One comment revealed that he had an inaccurate version of the story behind why his dad left in the first place.

"Nathan, where did you hear that?"

"School."

Who would say such a thing in front of Nathan? I
wanted names! I resisted the temptation to ask. Did I really want to know? People let things slip, and no one had
done it maliciously. It didn't matter whether he'd heard talk
from classmates who'd picked up half the truth or moms
chatting in the courtyard. He was bound to hear gossip
eventually. Now that he had, I needed to decide how much

truth to give him. He wasn't old enough for the details that Christian knew. Neither of them needed a full play-by-play.

When my husband originally moved out of the house, I told Nathan, "Dad has some things he needs to work on."

The memory of him crying still stung. "Why can't he work on them here?"

"There are some things that a person needs to deal with away from home."

It had taken a lot of courage to agree to a plan that included separation, and I'd hoped it would end in restoring our marriage. Everyone involved hoped for that. When it didn't, I had to explain why Dad wasn't coming home, again without divulging more than Nathan needed to know at such a young age. At times I worried that Christian knew too much.

Nathan sniffed. I prayed for the right words to clear up confusion and give him peace. *Help me know when to stop, Lord.*

I started with clearing up part of the story he'd heard that was flat-out wrong before moving on to the true parts. "Nate, Dad made some . . . choices. No one expected him to move away for good. I don't know why he did, but I do know he loves you and Christian. Everyone at your school and at church loves you too." I gave him another hug. "You have so many people who love you. God is taking good care of us."

He let out a shaky breath. I felt him relax.

That's enough for now. Getting his question answered and being reminded that he was loved was all he needed for today.

Someday he would have more complicated questions that would send me running to God for the right words. When that happened, I would pray for more wisdom to share just enough truth for the moment.

"Why can't Dad come home?" "Why aren't you and Dad married anymore?" "Is it true that . . . ?" "A girl at school said . . ."

We know to expect questions, but that doesn't make the big ones any easier. What if the truth includes details that our child isn't ready for? How do we tell our version of the story without putting down the father he or she loves? How should we handle it when clearing up confusion includes acknowledging that friends are discussing our situation within earshot of our kids? We don't want to say too much, but we don't want to lie to them either. What does God want us to say?

What questions are you still unsure how to answer right now? What have your kids heard that you now need to clear up? I pray that the truth of Proverbs 2:6—"For the LORD gives wisdom; from his mouth come knowledge and understanding"—will fill you with the confidence to seek Him for the exact words that will help your child feel secure. May He make it clear what needs to be said now and what needs to wait, and allow every awkward conversation to be driven by His love.

Lord, You tell me to be truthful, but there are some truths that my child isn't ready for yet. Remind me to seek You before answering difficult questions. Give me courage when honesty is hard and restraint when it will only do more damage. Thank You for guiding my words. Amen.

TO TAKE INTO YOUR DAY

Read: Proverbs 2:1–11

Consider: What questions are you dreading having to answer? What have you learned from saying too much?

Survival Tip: Talk to a single mom who is further down the path than you are and ask how she handled difficult questions.

19

The Scarlet Letter

When they kept on questioning him, he straightened up
and said to them, "Let any one of you who is
without sin be the first to throw a stone at her."

John 8:7

ONLY ONE PERSON IN THE ROOM knew I was going through a divorce, so I tried not to take the debate about divorced women in Christian leadership personally.

I focused on my knitting project, working my needles faster as my own inner debate raged on. Should I continue suffering in silence or risk making everyone uncomfortable by announcing, "*I'm* going through a divorce, and here's why"? Before my expression betrayed me, I set my project aside, picked up my snack plate, and casually left the room.

In Anne's kitchen I tried to shake off the wave of emotions. If those ladies knew what sent me away mid-discussion, they would feel bad and apologize. That didn't erase the humbling reminder that, regardless of how lovingly

I'd been surrounded over the past several months, soon I would be a divorced woman in the church. According to some, that should disqualify me from certain things regardless of the circumstances.

Anne joined me in the kitchen. "I suggested that we change topics to something less divisive."

"Thank you."

"I should have spoken up sooner. I'm sorry."

I squeezed her hand. "I appreciate you speaking up at all. Besides, they didn't know."

We drowned our sorrows in the guacamole I'd made, then returned to the living room to talk about crafts, yarn, and other non-divisive topics. Knitting gave me an excuse to be quiet.

I thought about my mother's grandmother, Anna, a woman I'd only met through pictures and stories. I'd grown up on the sad tale of Great-Grandpa Hugo deserting Anna and their nine children for another woman, back in the day when divorce came with a guaranteed stigma. Their whole church snubbed them. Mom's mother had been too young to remember how it felt to suddenly not be invited to birthday parties, but she vividly recalled the embarrassment of only having two dresses later as a preteen.

Since becoming a single mom, I'd felt a kinship with Great-Grandma Anna. How did she survive without child support? The thought of her church and friends turning their backs when she needed them most crushed me. She wouldn't have heard the discussion that sent me to the kitchen tonight because she wouldn't have been invited to the gathering.

I thanked God that my story looked very different from Anna's. If the worst I had to fear was possibly not serving in areas that, at the moment, I had no interest in anyway, I still had plenty to be grateful for. My sons weren't experiencing the isolation that wounded Grandma and her siblings so deeply that Mom didn't hear about it until she was pregnant with me. Regardless of how friends felt about who ought to serve where, they still talked to me, sat with me at church, had Nathan over for play dates, and gobbled up the guacamole I made for our get-togethers. I would go to church on Sunday knowing the congregation was waiting, not to throw stones at me or stick a scarlet *D* on my chest, but to love me like Jesus loved. Experiencing divorce first-hand was equipping me to model His grace in the future. I understood that each broken marriage had a unique story behind it that only God knew all the details of and real people He could use in any way He chose.

No matter what your story looks like, hopefully you have enough support to appreciate how far society has come in our treatment of single moms. We no longer live in the days when your child will be the only one in class whose parents are divorced, nor will you live under a cloud of humiliation.

Still, it hurts to know that a time might come when you will feel judged, labeled, or excluded. Will you spend the rest of your life explaining your situation and dreading the moment when people prove far less forgiving than Jesus was?

When comments trigger shame and fear, take comfort in the Lord, who even came to the defense of a woman caught in adultery. Ask Him for a tiny glimpse of His grace, just in allowing you to be a single mom now instead of a hundred years ago.

Lord, I know we have come a long way, but sometimes I still feel branded. Comfort me when insensitive words wound me. Thank You for extending Your grace to me. Amen.

TO TAKE INTO YOUR DAY

Read: John 8:1–11; Psalm 146

Consider: When have you felt judged or held back because of being a single mom? How has your experience made you aware of areas where you might have been judgmental in the past?

Survival Tip: Ask God to heighten your sensitivity toward women whom society snubs or rejects.

20

A Weekend with Dad

Do not be anxious about anything, but in every situation,
by prayer and petition, with thanksgiving,
present your requests to God.

Philippians 4:6

ONE OF *THOSE* WEEKENDS had arrived. My sons'
dad was coming to town. These visits did not take place
on a consistent basis, so they always felt awkward. While
Nathan enjoyed the required time with his father, Christian
was at an age where he could decide for himself whether he
wanted to see his dad or avoid him. I, on the other hand,
needed to get past the dread of walking Nathan to the car.

How was I supposed to act? Friendly? Cold? Silent?

What should I wear? Was it more appropriate to go
with "See what you did to me" frumpy or "Look what you
threw away" hot?

I did know that my attorney had advised me not to let
my husband in the house because it would be confusing

for the boys. The designated meeting place would be our crumbling driveway.

I rallied my prayer troop as the weekend approached and followed advice to fill the time with activities that would get my mind off being without Nathan. I had a movie set aside to watch from his "Worst Movies of All Time" list (films that feature pretty costumes and British accents), and planned to run errands and have coffee with a friend, then clean the house. Maybe I would start to look forward to these visits.

But as time ticked on toward Friday afternoon and I tried to accept this new routine of packing Nathan's suitcase and sending him off with the man who'd shattered my trust, anxiety gripped me all over again.

What if he didn't bring Nathan back?

What if, as Nathan got older, he decided Dad was more fun than I was?

What if Nathan got hurt?

What if he fed Nathan junk all weekend, then brought him home sick or in the throes of a sugar crash?

I can't do this!

Stop torturing yourself with what might happen, the voice of reason urged. *You* can *do this. You have to do this.*

But I'm so nervous and scared!

God gently assured me, *I know you are.*

I focused on how to make the drop-off and pickup as

smooth as possible. Nathan would not benefit from Mom freaking out. I thanked God that I didn't have to send him out the door with an abusive father or put him on an airplane alone. When had Nathan had anything but a good time with his dad?

When dread over seeing *him* gripped me once more, I asked God to help me be hospitable without crossing the line into fake-friendly. I made a point to look my best, not for my soon-to-be-ex-husband's sake, but for my own confidence.

The doorbell rang on Friday afternoon. *Father, help me.* Nathan rushed to the door. *Thank You that he is happy and eager.* I noted how his eyes sparkled when his dad commented that he'd gotten taller and needed a haircut. A surprising peace swept over me even in the awkwardness of standing in the driveway with someone I couldn't let through the door. *You can do this.*

By the time Nathan came home, healthy, happy, and in one piece, I thanked God that, with His help, I could survive these weekends with Dad.

"Do not be anxious about anything . . ." (Philippians 4:6) takes on a whole new meaning as we learn to adjust to a schedule that includes separation from our kids. Whether we can trust the father of our children or have reasons to worry, the anticipation can be our worst enemy. Yes, this is a part of life; yes, we will get used to it; yes, single moms across America send their children off with their dads all the time. But for now it's foreign and hard. How could God possibly expect a mom not to be anxious? How can we obey Him when the news, other women' stories, and our own imaginations give us countless reasons to fear? What does God expect from those who have legitimate concerns as they watch their children pile into Dad's car?

We get to a place of peace a lot more quickly when we honestly confess our fears to God, ask Him to ease them, recognize His divine ways of protecting kids, and begin to see the benefits of choosing to do our best to obey.

Heavenly Father, preparing to send my kids away even for a weekend and facing the man I once loved fill me with anxiety. You promise peace in exchange for my thanksgiving and prayers. Allow me to experience that as I trust You. Amen.

TO TAKE INTO YOUR DAY

Read: Philippians 4:6–9
Consider: What are your methods for making visitation drop-offs easier for yourself and your kids?
Survival Tip: List some fun or productive things that you can do while your children are with their dad.

21

Letting Him Have It

Fools give full vent to their rage,
but the wise bring calm in the end.

Proverbs 29:11

MY HEART PULSED WITH ANGER as I grabbed the phone to call my husband. Or was he my ex-husband? What was I supposed to call him now that a divorce petition had been filed?

"Don't be afraid to let him have it." A close friend's words echoed in my mind.

How many times had she encouraged me to get tougher? No matter what my sons' dad did or said, I never felt free to do that. A website suggested being "businesslike" while going through a divorce, so that's the approach I'd decided to take. But today's events had officially pushed me over the edge. I was done being polite or even businesslike.

I should have taken the tightness in my head, the

blurred thoughts, and my impulse to pace as warnings to cool off and pray. Instead, I barely got past hello before I started making use of my quick and creative way with words.

I hung up feeling so much better.

I called a friend to brag.

A truly explosive person would have called my outburst mild. I'd basically spoken the truth in a more intense tone than usual. But for a girl who'd only recently learned to say, "I feel angry today" without a sudden onslaught of guilt, it felt like a full-blown tantrum.

"Good for you," she said when I recapped the rather one-sided chat.

"See, I have a backbone."

So why did I feel like the worst version of me had just escaped from her cage?

Yes, I had a good reason to be upset. I knew there was such a thing as righteous anger. My friends had a point when they said I needed to be firm. But I sensed that God's idea of *firm* did not include spouting off and craving praise afterward. How would I respond the next time he did something to upset me?

I thought about my sons, who'd probably heard my rant. What kind of example did I set?

The reality that life now required me to learn how to deal with "my ex" hit once again. I thought about the many friends who were angry with the man who'd left me stranded. As satisfying as that felt, I was the one who had to make this changed relationship work over the long haul, and I was the one accountable to God for my behavior.

That was the day I made up my mind to let God decide how I should treat the father of my sons. From what I knew of God, He typically didn't encourage laying in to people. I needed to ask Him to help me stand strong when needed, but in a biblical way. In the end, I wanted my soon-to-be-former husband to look back and know I had held my ground without being rude, cruel, or vindictive. No matter what anyone else thought, I answered to God.

How are we supposed to act when the man we expected to love forever suddenly feels like the enemy? Dealing with frustrations related to dividing a shared life in two gets even more complicated when others offer well-intended opinions on how we should treat the one we no longer know how to behave around. As nice as it feels to have someone on our side cheering on our rants, God calls us to a different standard.

"Fools give full vent to their rage, but the wise bring calm in the end" (Proverbs 29:11). Is it possible to do this when we have a right to be mad, or when the other person is being unreasonable? It is when we learn to pause before speaking and ask our heavenly Father to stay close during conflict, guiding our words even as our hearts race.

Heavenly Father, some days I want so badly to let my anger rage on—to make him suffer. I confess that it feels good to know some of my friends hate him. Forgive me for that and for the times when I let my emotions rule the conversation. Help me face conflict with dignity and restraint, even when righteous anger is justified. Amen.

TO TAKE INTO YOUR DAY

Read: James 1:19–20

Consider: What difference might you make by keeping your anger under control?

Survival Tip: Find a healthy way to vent your frustrations, such as journaling or exercise.

22

On the Fifth Day of Christmas

Because of the LORD's great love we are not consumed,
for his compassions never fail.

Lamentation 3:22

I KEPT A SUNDAY SMILE on my face while singing with the worship team, then Jill gave me a hug after the service and I couldn't pretend anymore. The day before, I'd gotten through what would have been my husband's and my twenty-third anniversary, thanks to a group of friends who took me out for a long coffee date. We'd laughed, overdosed on caffeine and carbs, and talked about everything but the significance of the day. Later, I'd watched a funny movie with the boys to celebrate the two wonderful gems who had come from my marriage: Christian and Nathan.

Sunday morning arrived with a weight of repressed emotions and dread over facing the final week leading up to Christmas.

Jill sat with me, handed me tissue, and invited me and Nathan to go out to lunch with her family. I let myself rest that afternoon and thanked God for sending one group of friends to distract me from a painful day and another to comfort me when it was time to stop running from that pain.

Under the Christmas tree sat yet one more reminder that people understood how difficult this holiday season must be for me and my kids. An anonymous source had given us a 12 Days of Christmas box. We'd been instructed to open one package per day starting on December 14. So far the boys and I had unwrapped a new Christmas CD, two bottles of cider, three boxes of holiday bread mix, four bars of a natural soap I liked, and five packs of fun-shaped noodles. It didn't matter if the gifts were practical or frivolous; each one felt like a hug from Jesus. I wanted to thank someone, so I announced every gift on Facebook. Already I felt excitement building to find tomorrow's surprise and announce, "On the sixth day of Christmas our secret friend gave to us . . ."

All I'd hoped for was to get through the holiday season. Instead, even under the cloud of memories and knowing what we would never enjoy as a whole family again, a spirit of bittersweet joy filled our home. Jesus felt uniquely close to us as we prepared to celebrate His birth with a mix of usual traditions and doing some things differently. I recorded each reminder of His care as evidence that some-day Christian, Nathan, and I might look back on this Christmas as one of our most precious.

The flood of kindness moved me to consider someone else who was most likely having a hard Christmas—my soon-to-be-ex-husband's parents.

I should invite them over for Christmas Eve.

We always had. Why not this year too? They eagerly accepted. Instead of continuing our long-standing routine of attending the Christmas Eve service together and dreading how strange that would feel with one person missing, I made a nice dinner. When they stuck around to watch our favorite version of *A Christmas Carol* with us, I knew I'd done the right thing. From this Christmas on, things would be different, but that didn't mean holidays couldn't be filled with Christ's love.

Nothing resurrects the pain of separation like holidays. Eventually each of us must face Christmas, anniversaries, and a calendar full of other special days. While we long to get it over with and try to make the best of things, God occasionally surprises us by turning the bitterness sweet even in the agony of letting go of treasured traditions.

"Because of the LORD's great love we are not consumed, for his compassions never fail" (Lamentation 3:22).

Sometimes His compassion arrives in cards or anonymous gifts, or shows up through invitations to "Come to our house," or friends who make it okay for us not to be in a festive mood. He can also express love in an unexpected moment when we discover the beauty in making someone else's day a little better.

As you prepare for the next "God, just get me through this" holiday, ask Him to make His compassion real to you in whatever form He chooses.

Heavenly Father, the grief that holidays stir right now is almost impossible to describe. Thank You that I don't need to explain this to You, because You know every emotion before it hits. Thank You for the sweet ways that friends come close and send comfort. Help me to be sensitive to others who are also hurting at a time that used to be filled with celebration. Amen.

TO TAKE INTO YOUR DAY

Read: Lamentations 3:19–24

Consider: How has God shown you His love as you struggled to get through holidays as a single mom?

Survival Tip: Reach out to someone else who is experiencing a sad holiday, anniversary, or significant day.

23

Creepy Train Guy

My son, do not let wisdom and understanding out of your sight, preserve sound judgment and discretion.

Proverbs 3:21

THE OLDER MAN in the train station was probably guilty of oversharing, but he seemed lonely so I kept listening. Henry said he was a Christian and no longer had a family. I figured as soon as we boarded, my sons and I would go our way and he would go his.

Partway through the trip, Henry passed us in the lounge car. He patted my shoulder. *It has been a while since I did the guy/girl thing, but I'm pretty sure it's considered inappropriate for him to touch a strange woman, especially in front of her kids.* Still, I smiled.

After lunch, Nathan and Christian went to their seats with a bag of Skittles and a video game. I'd just lost myself in a battered paperback when Henry slipped into the seat beside me. He reeked of liquor.

Oh, no. Lord, make him go away!

He slurred a soliloquy about how fascinating he found me. He leaned closer. "You seem surprised that I'm interested in you."

I forced my voice to work. "You don't know me."

I'll confess that I felt flattered even in my discomfort. For the first time since my dating years, a man was flirting with me. A whiff of him brought me back to reality.

He rested his hand on my arm. "I've been watching you."

Ew!

I moved back so he was no longer touching me.

The porter walked by. *Should I flag her down?*

He went on about how beautiful and intelligent and special I was, and why he felt it was God's will that we spend time together. He called me *darling*. I knew I should ask him to leave but couldn't find the words. *God, help! Rescue me!*

I told Henry I was married.

"This isn't a relationship that would come between you and your husband."

Which version of the Bible did he read?

I pointed out my sons. He acted shocked that I could have a son Christian's age.

Oh, please.

The train couldn't reach our stop fast enough.

He stood on shaky, alcohol-affected legs. "Give me a call sometime."

I reached for my carry-on, then straightened my shoulders. "It was nice to meet you." (Said like, "*Don't count on it.*")

We'd barely exited the train before Christian blurted out, "What was that?"

Nathan nudged me. "*Darling.*"

Creepy Train Guy was the talk of our vacation. Nathan seized every opportunity to call me *darling*, my sobering reminder that he and Christian had watched a dirty old man hit on their mom.

Why hadn't God answered my prayer?

Maybe you had something to learn.

I recapped the story to my friend Teri.

"He sounds like a predator."

That word sent a colder chill through me than Henry's touch. The discussion confirmed my vulnerable state. I was naïve, needy, easily swayed by sob stories, and totally out of practice when it came to men.

Thank You for protecting me, God. Even if Henry wasn't dangerous, he clearly lacked boundaries. So had I, right in front of my boys. It was time to ask God to help me come up with a plan for protecting myself from the Henrys of the world.

Rule #1: No talking to lonely old men.

"Preserve sound judgment and discretion," Proverbs 3:21 urges. You may have already needed giant amounts of both as you learned the importance of boundaries. Sometimes it takes a bad experience to teach us that being without a husband opens us up to unwanted attention.

Proverbs promises that wisdom will keep us safe. While we don't want to be paranoid or assume that every man who smiles at us is making a pass, it's important to understand our vulnerability, both for our own sakes and our children's. As you go into a world filled with both unsafe and perfectly good people, ask God to be your Protector and your source of discernment.

Lord, help me be wise as I relearn how to deal with the opposite sex. Give me the words and the courage to be assertive when needed, and the good sense to set boundaries. Amen.

TO TAKE INTO YOUR DAY

Read: Proverbs 3:21–26

Consider: What makes you vulnerable with the opposite sex?

Survival Tip: Make a plan for protecting yourself and your kids from uncomfortable situations. For example, come up with a code that means, "We need to get away from this person."

24

Before the Judge

For God will bring every deed into judgment,
including every hidden thing, whether it is good or evil.

Ecclesiastes 12:14

I HAD NEVER FELT SO SMALL and insignificant in my life. The judge towered over the courtroom like we were in a cartoon. This was only a case management conference, but my heart raced as if I were on trial. *I can't imagine what I'd feel like if I'd done something wrong.*

As soon as the judge hears my side of things, she'll order what my sons and I need. Instead, I got my first lesson in what it meant to face the family court system.

The judge called me by name, but the longer she spoke, the more clearly I saw myself as I imagined she did—as a case number. My attorney cared about all of my concerns and needs, but even she knew certain details wouldn't matter. We lived in a no-fault-divorce state, where every debt and asset was community property, child and spousal support depended on income only, and both parents had rights regardless of their choices.

One detail jumped out to the judge: My husband's income would make it difficult for her to order spousal support, while I was legally blind and might qualify for SSI (a form of Social Security for the blind and visually impaired). I explained why that would prevent me from building my freelancing income. She recommended I apply anyway. I felt even smaller.

A look at our debt prompted her to advise pursuing bankruptcy while my husband and I were still legally married.

I'm going to be divorced, possibly on SSI, and bankrupt? I almost gave in to tears right there. *If she really knew me and heard the whole story, she . . . she might do the exact same thing.* Her goal was to settle our case according to what she saw on paper. She probably thought she was doing me a favor.

Talk of money got set aside for the sensitive topics of custody and visitation. My husband had agreed that I should have primary physical custody with shared legal custody, but we had yet to agree on a realistic visitation plan that I felt comfortable with. As the judge attempted to put my fears to rest, I got hit with the soul-wrenching realization that my comfort level wouldn't be a deciding factor.

God, do we matter to the court at all?

I knew that none of the judge's decisions were personal. I was at the mercy of a system that didn't have time to care about anything beyond the imperfect policies of our state.

After Nathan and Christian went to bed that night, I unleashed the injustices of the day to God, every reason why that judge should care more.

A moment of calm washed over me when I remembered whom I was talking to. He knew every detail and exactly what my sons and I needed. *I have seen everything that happened from the day your story unfolded*, He reminded me, *and I do care. I'm a fair Judge. I'm bigger than the system.*

All I could do was believe the assurance that God had a window into my case that the judge and even my caring attorney lacked—full knowledge. No matter how our future got mapped out on court documents, the perfect Judge had the power to make things right.

———

You probably don't need to be told that our system is broken. It's possible that you've already cried many nights over decisions that went the exact opposite of what you had hoped for. It's likely that judges care far more than they appear to when they make decisions that will affect our kids and us for years to come, but on the surface they seem heartless and laws often don't make sense.

Our only hope for avoiding complete despair is to place our fragile trust in the God of perfect justice, even when our situation is at its bleakest. We can remember that, while He doesn't promise we won't suffer, His Word is filled with evidence that righteous justice comes eventually. Take some time to pour out your case to the God who cares about every detail of it.

Lord, I don't understand our system, or why You seem to sit back and allow unfairness. Help me trust You when I feel powerless. Help me remember that You have ways of working behind the scenes and bringing justice when we least expect it. Help me trust Your plan. Amen.

TO TAKE INTO YOUR DAY

Read: Psalm 33

Consider: How has God shown you that His justice is greater than the system?

Survival Tip: Form a small team of friends to pray you and your kids through the legal process.

25

Under a Microscope

Where can I go from your Spirit?
Where can I flee from your presence?

Psalm 139:7

"I HAVEN'T SEEN YOUR HUSBAND at church lately. Has he been working weekends?"

I toyed with the emerald on my wedding ring finger that announced to the observant, *No longer attached.* "He left over the summer."

With every passing week more people knew my business. I couldn't decide how I felt about that.

I understood that it was better for people to know the truth than wonder and speculate. However, I also had two sons to protect. We attended a relatively small church that functioned like a family. Being in the choir and on the worship team put me in the spotlight. Already I'd discovered that being surrounded by support meant occasionally feeling like my sons and I were living under a microscope.

Getting much-needed financial assistance meant sharing my budget and income. Asking for rides meant friends saw my kids at their best and at their worst. One minute it comforted me to know some women wanted to slap my husband silly and the next I wanted to defend the man I'd loved enough to marry and have children with. I appreciated that Christian and Nathan had so many surrogate moms and dads, as long as those moms and dads didn't analyze their emotional responses, critique their behavior or chore lists, or correct them.

Would it always be this way?

One day I had lunch with my friend Teri. Her marriage had miraculously survived a betrayal that would have torn most couples apart, and she regularly shared her story to encourage other women. She knew my whole saga. Teri seemed like the right person to express my concerns to and ask, "How did your family move forward?"

"Honestly?" I detected the *"You probably don't want to hear this"* look she gave me. "We had to move."

Move? We'll never do that. Our support system is here.

If I'm going to stay where I am and thrive, I need to stop being so hyper-sensitive, I told myself.

Times of pouring out my frustrations to God reminded me that my sons and I probably *were* under a microscope in some ways. That came with becoming a single mom in a tight-knit community. I needed to get used to the idea that whether we stayed put or moved, there would always be someone observing me and my sons and deciding what our lives ought to look like. People watched us because they cared. Anyone who judged me answered to God. When friends crossed the line, I needed to learn to either speak up or give them the benefit of the doubt and let it go.

Remember: I'm watching you too, God instilled on my heart. *I have every one of My children under a very loving microscope. Focus on Me.* The words of Psalm 139 became a regular reminder of my Father's watchfulness as He continued to pour out His love through His people.

"You have searched me, LORD, and you know me. You know when I sit and when I rise; you perceive my thoughts from afar" (Psalm 139:1–2). When we are going through a life-altering process, it can feel like everyone is watching and critiquing us. In reality, people probably aren't observing us as closely as our tender hearts try to convince us they are. Our loving heavenly Father, on the other hand, watches us constantly.

He knows every detail of how you got to where you are and how desperately you want life to feel normal again. He understands your fears and up-and-down emotions. He completely gets why, as mad as you are at your ex-husband, it still hurts when friends bash him. He knows how embarrassing it is to have to explain why he isn't with you anymore when you see friends who haven't heard the news yet.

In moments when you feel like you and your kids are living under a microscope, picture yourself under the watchful eye of the Father, who follows you through every moment of every day. Ask Him to help you care more about what He sees than what others might be thinking.

Heavenly Father, thank You for the assurance I have in a God who sees everything. Thank You for putting people in my life who care enough to watch out for me and my children. Lift the weight of self-consciousness so I can feel Your love. Amen.

TO TAKE INTO YOUR DAY

Read: Psalm 139

Consider: What are the frustrations of feeling like you're under a microscope?

Survival Tip: Seek the wisdom of a friend who has survived an ordeal similar to yours.

26

God, I Don't Belong Here

Every good and perfect gift is from above,
coming down from the Father of the heavenly lights,
who does not change like shifting shadows.

James 1:17

HOW HAD I ENDED UP in the welfare office? I'd fought so hard to avoid this. I was applying for Medicaid, not food stamps or financial assistance, but it was still the welfare office, and I felt a little too good for this place. If not for the kindness of others, I would be on all three services already. That didn't lessen the degradation of knowing I qualified for any program that might cause people to assume things about me and my kids.

Phrases like *entitlement program*, *welfare mom*, and *below poverty level* felt like cruel brands searing away my sense of self. I wanted every person in that office to know how hard I worked, that I had a college degree, that I had just enough in my bank account not to qualify for SSI, and I was only there because it would be unwise to risk the possibility of paying for an ER visit out-of-pocket. I'd purposely worn an outfit that told everyone in the room, "I don't belong here."

Friends had attempted to ease the blow. "Single moms are what government programs were created for. If my tax dollars can go toward helping you, then that makes me happy."

I tried to be happy too, but as I got one step closer to the desk, I just felt trashy.

What are you saying about the other women in this line? I asked myself. *That they are trashy? What a mean thing to imply. How many of them do you think are just dying to be here today? Which of them included "Be on Welfare" on her list of goals?*

The thought stopped me in my It's-all-about-what-people-think-of-me tracks.

According to the income chart, I did belong there. My husband's series of medical problems years earlier had taught me how quickly one trip to the hospital could devastate a family's finances. How noble was it to allow pride to stand in the way of something I no longer had through a spouse's employment benefits?

Think of this place as one more way that God is providing.

Hadn't He told His people to provide for the poor? If every good thing came from Him, didn't that include Medicaid?

I drew strength from that thought and the presence of my friend Julie, who'd given me a ride and knew how desperately I didn't want to be there. I would turn in my paperwork, hopefully make the clerk's day in some way, walk out with my head high, thank God for placing me in a society that had things like Medicaid, then vent with Julie privately. I didn't want this, but I qualified, and at least for now, I couldn't afford to go without it.

Even those of us with college educations and impressive résumés can find ourselves taking a number, spending an afternoon in a long line, and handing in forms that label us *poor*. As if divorce isn't humiliating enough!

While we allow God to humble us (*How many times had I judged those on welfare?*), it also helps to remember that since ancient times, He has called people to provide for those in need. As much as our vanity hates the idea of handouts, our well-being might depend on them. God provides in a number of ways, including the government. The best thing we can do for ourselves and our kids is see every resource as a gift from our caring Father, apply for what we need, and remind ourselves repeatedly that it won't be forever.

Heavenly Father, forgive me for thinking I'm above certain kinds of assistance. Help me be grateful rather than resentful. Remind me that my worth is not diminished by the services I qualify for. Thank You for providing, even in ways I wish I didn't need. Amen.

TO TAKE INTO YOUR DAY

Read: Leviticus 19:9–10; 25:35–38; Psalm 140:12–13

Consider: Which services have you avoided out of pride?

Survival Tip: If you qualify for a government resource and know you need it for a period of time, give yourself the okay to apply. Ask a supportive friend to go with you.

27

Father Figures

Father to the fatherless, defender of widows—this is God,
whose dwelling is holy.

Psalm 68:5 NLT

NATHAN'S INFECTIOUS LAUGH rang through the church narthex. My friend Kathy's husband, Howard, had grabbed him in a playful headlock.

"Howard," Kathy scolded. "Leave him alone."

Howard let go, only to challenge Nathan to arm wrestling. "He's a boy. It's good for him."

A smile cracked Nathan's attempt at an angry snarl as he pushed against Howard's strength. His eyes widened in determination.

Kathy nudged me. "Look at him. He's loving it."

Howard let Nathan win once but not twice. He tousled Nate's hair and fist-bumped him.

I laughed. *"Father to the fatherless . . ."* Obviously Howard wasn't God, but our heavenly Father was using him and other men to fill the void that Nathan and Christian's dad had left, including the need to wrestle. *Thank You, Lord.*

The previous week Howard had come over to the house while I was at worship team practice and helped Christian fix the lock on our back gate. I'd been grateful enough for that, but when he also took both boys out for ice cream afterward and engaged Christian in a long talk, I couldn't thank him or God enough.

Couples like Howard and Kathy and our many other friends were soothing the ache of watching my sons go through life without a dad and no longer having a whole family. A skit that I'd watched at a retreat, illustrating how Jesus takes over the father role in homes like mine, had filled me with relief. But what about the everyday stuff? Each time Christian and Nathan sat through another chick flick with me I feared they'd be wrecked. How would throwing the ball around with his legally blind mom affect Nathan's future in sports? I tried to stay consistent with nightly devotional times, encouraged the boys to see God as their father, and had always been one to bring Him into daily conversations ("Wasn't it nice of God to create so many yummy foods for us to enjoy?"). But was that enough? Seeing happy intact families, especially those with strong father figures, added to the regret over what my sons lacked. Who would finish guiding Christian into adulthood? Who would usher Nate into the teen years?

Witnessing Nathan's male-bonding moment with Howard reminded me that God had creative ways of making up for the absence of an earthly dad. My sons no longer had a traditional family, but they had more godly men in their lives than two young guys could ask for. While I did my best to raise them to love, serve, and trust their heavenly Father, He would make up the difference, both through His people and in moments that only He and Christian or Nathan witnessed. No matter what had happened with their dad, they would never be left fatherless.

Even if your child spends some time with his or her dad, there might be moments when your heart breaks over the holes left by not having him available on a daily basis. You do your best, but you are only one person, and there are some things that require a guy.

This is when we have the opportunity to see God play the role of Father to the fatherless. As we teach our children to go to Him with their needs and model trust as we call on Him daily, we might also see Him send father figures through friends and family members. In the process, He can also meet our need to feel like part of a family as we join friends for activities, holidays, or just having someone to sit with in church.

"Father to the fatherless, defender of widows—this is

God, whose dwelling is holy. God places the lonely in families . . ." (Psalm 68:5–6). How has He done this for your children?

Heavenly Father, it makes me sad to think about all my children are missing out on by not having a dad around all the time. There are some things that I can't make up for. Thank You for being a Father to the fatherless. Let me see You bring father figures into my children's lives. Teach us a new meaning of family. Amen.

TO TAKE INTO YOUR DAY

Read: Psalm 68:4–19
Consider: How have you seen God be a Father to your children? How has He provided father figures?
Survival Tip: Find an activity that will connect your children with godly male role models.

28

Messed Up

And not only this, but we also exult in our tribulations,
knowing that tribulation brings about perseverance.

Romans 5:3 *NASB*

NATHAN PROUDLY WALKED UP to the front of the sanctuary where his school held chapel. He was one of six students receiving the President's Award for earning straight As for the school year. I trembled with pride and joy. This was not supposed to be happening!

Both of my sons did well in school. From the day Nathan entered kindergarten wearing his fresh white polo shirt and navy shorts, he'd been eager to learn and get good grades. He was one of those toddlers who amazed adults with his quick mastery of the ABC puzzle and appearing to read because he had memorized his favorite books. Earning the President's Award had been his goal since the principal had announced it. Why was I so surprised to see the kid who'd once cried over missing two words on a spelling test living up to his own standards?

I guess I'd heard one too many stories about children of single moms struggling in school. There Nathan stood, defying those odds, proving himself to be a boy who persevered even when life threw curves. Christian was at home getting ready for his job at a local museum, a position at which he excelled. He spent a large chunk of his off-hours helping me with Nathan, doing small repairs around the house, and making use of his love of cooking by planning and preparing dinner once a week.

For some reason I remembered a funny photo I once had on my desktop, showing a kitten sitting on a book, with the caption, "I read your journal. You are messed up!" I related to the fear of being exposed as the emotional mess I felt like sometimes. Today, as I watched Nathan march back to his seat with his friends and waited to snap pictures of him with his award, I marveled over how messed up he wasn't. How many times had I worried that he and Christian would be ruined forever by the events of this past year and all that had led up to it? Instead, they continued to thrive.

My smile faded. What about down the road? Would Christian resent the many ways he had to fill in as the man of the house? Were problems with Nathan only being postponed until, say, middle school?

Don't think about that, I told myself. *Enjoy this moment.* I had a firm enough grip on reality to understand that each of us would be left a little messed up. How could we not be? I kept a close watch on my sons for signs of distress. But ruined forever? If Nathan could get to the end of his first school year after his father left with straight As, and if Christian could respond to this crisis by succeeding at his job and being helpful at home, they would be okay. What I saw happening was a picture of God's grace at work, possibly even a sign that they would be stronger men for what they'd had to persevere through.

———

When we consider all that our children have experienced, it's natural to worry about their futures. Will they fail in school or have behavior problems? Will they spend the rest of their lives in therapy? Kids are resilient, but a family crisis also takes its toll after a while. What will that look like? How resilient can we expect them to be when we are having a hard enough time as adults?

Then we watch our children soar in spite of all they've endured and see that verses like Romans 5:3 apply to them. They are hurting but persevering. With God and you at their sides, this experience may scar them but also strengthen them.

As we see tribulation bring about perseverance in us, we can have confidence that the same will be true for our kids.

Lord, my children didn't ask for any of this, but they are suffering for it anyway. I am so afraid they will be permanently injured. Thank You for being bigger than statistics, my fears, or even today's struggles. Be close to them today. Help them persevere. Amen.

TO TAKE INTO YOUR DAY

Read: Romans 5:1–5

Consider: Whose life reminds you that children of single moms can grow into successful men and women?

Survival Tip: Start praying specifically for your children's future. Ask friends to pray as well.

29

"Do Something!"

Let us therefore come boldly to the throne of grace, that we may obtain mercy and find grace to help in time of need.

Hebrews 4:16 NKJV

HOW COULD THIS BE HAPPENING? Why now? A week before our case settlement conference, I got some news that I knew would change everything. The job for which my husband had moved away had fallen through. He had a new employer but made less money. This would probably postpone the settlement conference and would definitely reduce my already-low support. A lot.

How could my sons and I live on less money?

I tried to distract myself with Bible study homework instead of screaming without concern for the neighbors.

"Come boldly to the throne of grace . . ."

I clenched my teeth. *Boldly? Really? Because I'm pretty upset.* I rested my head on my arms. A picture came to mind of God on His throne supposedly caring about my pitiful situation getting worse. I recalled a phase that both my sons went through as preschoolers when they caught on that I couldn't see well and decided there must be a connection between my ability to see and my ability to hear. If they really wanted my attention, they gently took hold of my face and pulled it very close to theirs.

The invitation from Hebrews echoed in my mind, and for the first time in months I felt like being bold. According to friends and pastors, God could handle my anger. *"How long, O Lord?"* Which psalm did that verse belong to again? I decided it didn't matter. If David could unleash his anguish to the Lord, so could I. I remembered enough to know it ended with him secure in God's goodness, not zapped by lightning.

I imagined myself approaching heavy, ornate double doors, grabbing two carved handles with the recommended boldness, and bursting in. Like a desperate child, I rushed across the shiny floor until I reached the throne where my heavenly Father sat. I grabbed hold of His robe. "Wake up!"

I waited to be scolded, *"Do you have any idea whom you're talking to?"* Instead, I sensed the same love that I'd felt for Christian and Nathan when their tiny hands cupped my cheeks and drew me close enough to see the intent in their eyes. I buried my face and fists into His chest. "Do something!"

Should I be more specific? Or maybe I didn't need to be. I rested there in His comfort, in the wonder that He would give it after I had behaved like a three-year-old, knowing how faithful He'd been already. I didn't finish my Bible study that day, but I left the throne room with the grace and help God had promised. I won't claim that I stopped fearing for the future, or that I didn't need to ask friends to pray because I felt confident enough about God's plan to not require any. I just knew God would do *something*. Months of paid bills and full cupboards in a house that we should have been kicked out of long ago proved that. For as long as this lasted, I could approach the throne at any time to meet with my Father and receive His grace.

"How long, O Lord? Will You forget me forever?" (Psalm 13:1 NKJV). When was the last time you felt these words? Last week? Yesterday? Five minutes ago? How often have you felt abandoned, forgotten, and forsaken, and wondered if God heard the conversation you had with your attorney or ex-husband or employer or whoever else made it possible for things to get worse?

"How long must I wrestle with my thoughts and day after day have sorrow in my heart?" (Psalm 13:2). Good question, right?

Each one of these moments allows us to take Him up

on His offer to welcome us into His throne room to pour out our anguish like David did so many times. Emptying our honest thoughts and emotions makes room for memories of His faithful history and a soothing presence that hopefully leaves us trusting in our Father's unfailing love.

Heavenly Father, sometimes it seems like the hard parts will drag on forever. Thank You for inviting me into Your presence even when I do nothing but complain. Help me trust Your faithfulness. Amen.

TO TAKE INTO YOUR DAY

Read: Psalm 13

Consider: What situation has your heart crying to God, "Do something"?

Survival Tip: Spend some time sharing your thoughts with God.

SECTION 4

finding my way

30

Standing Firm

Whoever walks in integrity walks securely,
but whoever takes crooked paths will be found out.

Proverbs 10:9

USUALLY I WOULD BE THRILLED to find two checks in the mail, but three days before a bankruptcy attorney was scheduled to file our paperwork, this felt like the worst possible timing. The checks needed to be reported as assets.

"Don't deposit them yet," one friend insisted. "You need that money to live on."

Her advice made sense, except that the attorney had specifically told me uncashed checks counted as income. I'd had to list everything from the funds in my IRA to the cash in my purse. My soon-to-be-ex-husband had to do the same. I didn't have control over his honesty, but I was responsible for my own.

"It is so close to the filing date," another friend said. "They won't know when the checks arrived."

But I knew. I had made a firm commitment to handle every step of the divorce, including the bankruptcy, with integrity. Suddenly the reality of what that might mean made me mad.

Why would God provide much-needed money only to have it sucked away by a bankruptcy I'd never wanted? Did He expect me to be so transparent that I reported income that arrived this close to zero hour?

My friends will be upset with me if I report this money and lose it. I'm scraping by as it is.

But I wouldn't be able to stand the guilt if I hid it. As deeply as my friends cared about my need to have the money for food, bills, and school clothes, they weren't the ones who had to swear I'd reported everything accurately. I didn't want to be the mom who covered the truth, got caught, and then had to explain that to my sons.

I knew what the book of James said: "If anyone, then, knows the good they ought to do and doesn't do it, it is sin for them" (4:17). I also knew God rewarded those who chose to do the right thing. God had asked me to live above reproach. He had honored my attempts up to this point and provided beyond expectations through this entire ordeal. Would I give up on His faithfulness now, or seize this opportunity to trust it and do what I knew was correct? In my heart I knew that, as much as we needed the money, my sons needed an example of integrity more. If I let others sway me against my conscience this time, how would I ever be able to stand firm in my convictions as a mother?

So I reported the income. If anyone asked about the checks, I would tell them I'd done exactly what I felt God wanted me to do. Wouldn't they want me to obey God?

Those funds went untouched. On the surface it seemed cruel of God to allow money to arrive just in time to provide additional stress. Looking back, though, I understand how badly I needed to be faced with the choice to obey God over the advice of friends as I learned to do what was best for my family.

Running a household alone offers plenty of practice in choosing whose voice to listen to. The law tells us what we must do, friends encourage us to fudge details for our own protection, and God tells us to do what is right even if it hurts. In all the injustice of our situation, why not protect what's ours?

In the end we must decide whether we are going to live with integrity or do what we can get away with, be honest or hide what we think we can't afford to lose.

As unfair as our system is, we trust a God who honors obedience. Today, no matter what decisions you are facing, ask Him to show you the correct thing to do and give you the courage to live a picture of integrity.

Lord, help me do what is right even when others try to pull me toward a supposedly safer direction. Show me that You honor obedience. When I seem to be paying a price for it, give me the strength to do the right thing anyway. Amen.

TO TAKE INTO YOUR DAY

Read: Job 27:4–6; Psalm 15

Consider: When has God rewarded your willingness to be honest even when it might cost you something?

Survival Tip: Write out a few Bible verses in your journal or on 3 x 5 cards that remind you of God's promise to honor integrity.

～ 31 ～

A Real Job

Whatever you do, work at it with all your heart,
as working for the Lord, not for human masters.

Colossians 3:23

"I THINK I NEED to get a real job," I told one of my friends.

"You get quite a bit of work now, don't you?"

"Not enough to support us once we leave this house."

I thanked God continually for sending enough freelance writing and editing jobs to cover my bills so I didn't need as much help from the church. However, I also wasn't paying a mortgage. The judge's temporary order included child support for Nathan but no alimony, and it would probably stay that way. I could not expect to pay rent on an unpredictable income. Love for my work had gotten tangled up with worry and guilt that I was failing as a breadwinner.

Since my husband had left, I'd brainstormed multiple job ideas. I now regretted not getting my master's degree or teaching credentials so I could qualify to teach more than adult education writing workshops. My first career of teaching preschool, subbing, and working in after-school programs was not something I wanted to return to. It had been fun at one time, but some frustrating low-paying jobs revealed that my gifts lay elsewhere.

"I guess at some point I'll have to take whatever I can get." And try not to loathe every moment of it.

"Whatever you do, work at it with all your heart, as working for the Lord" . . . I didn't know whether to feel inspired or annoyed by Colossians 3:23 coming to mind in such a timely manner. Of course I would have to accept whatever employment God provided, be thankful for it, and have a good attitude. I just didn't want His choice to include work I merely tolerated. At least I had more options than, say, Fantine in *Les Misérable*. Talk about a desperate single mom!

My friend cut off my inner whine fest. "I think you're doing what you're supposed to right now. Your kids need you. God is providing, and He'll provide when you have rent to pay. You do have a real job. You're a freelancer and you're a mom."

I thanked God for these words long after my friend and I parted. Maybe writer/mom was the job I needed to work at with all my heart right now, trusting that I served a wonderful Boss who knew how much income I needed now and in the future. He also knew how much I could hold on my plate at one time.

Thank You, Lord, that I am able to keep doing what I love and be home for my kids, I prayed. *Whatever job You provide in the future, help me work at it as joyfully as I do this one.*

Going from two incomes to only one leaves us feeling like we'll never earn enough no matter how many jobs we have. Verses like Colossians 3:23 might stir mixed emotions as you try to figure out how to pay your bills, care for your kids, and not resent how you got to this place. The search for work can be even more frustrating when we face the possibility of setting personal dreams aside.

Whatever your situation is—whether you are able to stay home with your kids or keep your current job, if you had to change jobs, or if you must take extra work just to keep the bills paid—ask God to reveal blessings in it. Ask Him to direct you to the path that will cover all of your needs, including your children's need to have you available to them. "Work at it with all your heart" becomes easier with time as we begin to see His purpose in where He has us.

Lord, I need to earn an income, but I also need to be there for my children. I have bills to pay, and I also have goals and desires. Help me, Father, to do today's work as if it's for You. Amen.

TO TAKE INTO YOUR DAY

Read: Matthew 6:31–34

Consider: How is God providing for your needs *now*? How is He making it possible for you to be there for your kids?

Survival Tip: If you are looking for a job, ask friends to keep an eye out for one that will be a good fit for you and your children.

32

"You Should Start Dating"

Take delight in the LORD, and he will give you the desires of your heart.

Psalm 37:4

SHERRY FINISHED trimming my hair, styled it with gel, and handed me a mirror. "You look so cute."

Susan walked over for a peek. "She does!"

Sherry removed the cape from around my shoulders. "We need to get you out there on a date."

I laughed.

"Stop that! You're a catch."

Susan wrapped a sisterly arm around me. "I know you don't feel like one right now, but you really are. Be careful about making it public that you're single."

I felt myself blush. "Yeah, right." I admired my fresh haircut. For a moment I felt like a catch.

Sherry swept the floor. "Why not join a Christian dating site?"

I reminded Sherry of one important fact: "I'm not single until my divorce is final."

"That's true. Well, when you're free, get out there, girl."

I pictured myself on a date, feeling as clueless as I had at seventeen when I went to a movie with a boy for the first time. After that came a series of boyfriends that I now referred to as a glaring reflection of low self-esteem, not because they were bad, but because I stuck with them regardless of how they treated me. I had embarrassing between-boyfriend memories of going to parties with big '80s hair, longing for a nice, cute guy to pay attention to me. The idea of entering the adult dating scene scared me to death. Had I learned nothing from Creepy Train Guy?

On the drive home I admitted to Susan, "I probably won't date for a while. It was never one of my gifts."

"Oh, we were just teasing. Christian and Nathan don't need you bringing men home. Kids get attached. I heard a radio psychologist tell a woman to wait until her children grew up."

I'd grown up with a girl whose divorced mom jumped from boyfriend to dysfunctional boyfriend. As predicted, my friend followed the same pattern.

But if I waited until Nathan reached adulthood, that meant being alone for a really long time!

A long time to figure out how not to repeat past mistakes. A long time to decide what kind of man I wanted to let into my life and learn what a godly man looked like. A long time to figure out what I needed to change in order to never settle for less than God's best.

For today, it felt good to know Sherry and Susan saw me as a catch. As strongly as I felt God urging me to postpone dating and let Him decide when I was ready, He'd used my friends' encouragement to remind me that I was still beautiful and valuable.

The pressure to enter the dating scene can hit long before we're ready. Friends want us to be happy. We miss feeling desirable, the fun of going out to movies and dinner with a man, the warmth of holding hands. Then come the memories of mistakes and bad dating choices, settling for less than God's perfect man, or thinking we had him only to lose him. Scenes from the past, along with the reality of all we've been through, remind us how wounded we really are, and why it might be wise to live life single for a while.

Having kids who need the security of our presence can keep us grounded as we wait for God to fulfill our true heart's desire. In the meantime, we have a gift of time to figure out what that desire really is, focus on our children, recover, learn who we are, and discover a sense of value that goes deeper than a date.

Heavenly Father, I admit that I want to feel beautiful and special. But I'm not ready to date, and my kids might not be ready to see me with a man who isn't their father for a while. Help me be patient, Lord. Show me what needs healing and where my value really lies as I wait on Your timing. Amen.

TO TAKE INTO YOUR DAY

Read: Psalm 37:3–6

Consider: How much pressure do you feel to date? What do you sense God telling you to do?

Survival Tip: Share your honest struggles about dating and men with God. Ask Him to reveal some benefits of waiting until both you and your children are ready.

~ 33 ~

On the Altar

"Fear not, for I am with you; be not dismayed,
for I am your God. I will strengthen you, yes, I will help you,
I will uphold you with My righteous right hand."

Isaiah 41:10 *NKJV*

SUMMER WAS ALMOST UPON US, when Nathan's dad could take him for more than a weekend to his home several hours away. No plans had been made yet, but anticipating a long separation from my youngest child loomed over me like a crushing anvil. Dad was responsible for finding child care, and I would be expected to trust his choice.

I pictured my son spending long days with a babysitter who only saw him as a source of cash, or at a summer program filled with kids he didn't know. What if the babysitter or those kids were mean to him?

Since his first Sunday in the nursery, Nathan's world had

been predictable and safe. He went to school and church with most of the same children. I was in choir, on the worship team, and attended a prayer group with many of his teachers. We spent vacations with Grandma, Grandpa, and cousins. His babysitters included his brother, grandparents, and church friends. Even though I knew his dad would never harm Nate, he had a new circle of friends I'd never met.

I'd encountered plenty of well-adjusted boys and girls who'd survived and even enjoyed summer visits with their dads. Why did I have to be such a drama queen? Maybe I could find a writers' conference to attend while Nate was gone or . . .

No! God, no! Nathan needs to be with me and Christian!

I thought about calling a friend to pray me down from the cliff but decided I didn't want to. They would only remind me to trust God, or share about someone they knew who'd had to allow visitation with a father who *really* couldn't be trusted. I didn't want to be reminded about Abraham laying his precious son, Isaac on the altar or Hannah keeping her vow to God to allow Samuel to be raised in the temple. None of that would comfort me. Nathan wasn't Abraham's or Sarah's or some other woman's son. He was my child. Horror stories I'd heard only made it more difficult to entrust him even to God.

As I gave in to helplessness, I knew I couldn't afford to. I was bound to a court system that I couldn't count on but must obey. I didn't spend enough time with Nathan's dad anymore to know whether I could trust his judgment or not, but so far God had proven Himself capable.

"Fear not, for I am with you; be not dismayed, for I am your God. I will strengthen you, yes, I will help you, I will uphold you with My righteous right hand" (Isaiah 41:10 NKJV).

I needed to trust that the Lord would strengthen me no matter what the summer brought, and that He would equip Nathan. Obeying the "Fear not" part would take a while, but I was counting on His ability to uphold me until this got easier.

Anticipating long separations from our children brings on anxiety that feels impossible to soothe. A weekend or half the week is one thing, but weeks at a time? So much can happen in a week or two weeks or half the summer! In the end, we have no alternative but to lay our precious sons and daughters on the altar like Abraham did and trust God to return them to us unharmed.

Isaiah 41:10 might feel easier read than done right now. No matter how legitimate your reservations are, ask your heavenly Father for assurance of His ability to strengthen and uphold you as you learn to trust Him with your children.

Heavenly Father, I love my children and do not want to be without them. Help me shut off my imagination and believe that they will be okay, because they have the best Father in the world looking out for them. Amen.

TO TAKE INTO YOUR DAY

Read: Psalm 46
Consider: What do you dread most about being separated from your kids for long periods of time?
Survival Tip: Avoid movies, conversations, and reading stories that will only feed your fears.

34

Depleted

Have mercy on me, LORD, for I am faint.

Psalm 6:2

JULIE PULLED INTO MY DRIVEWAY after giving me a ride home from Bible study. "Are you doing okay? You seem off today."

I picked up my purse and tote bag. They felt heavier than usual. Why did I feel teary? Nothing upsetting had happened beyond the usual. *What's wrong with me?* "I feel so worn out and out of sorts lately."

Everything took extra effort. Did I need to see a doctor? I felt like a two-year-old who'd gone without her nap—emotional, unfocused, irritable, grumpy with my sons, and suddenly useless when it came to keeping up with the demands of life. *God, I cannot afford to feel this way*, I prayed constantly, only to become more depleted. During an important phone call, I stumbled over my words and repeated myself. I didn't have the energy to care about dishes in the sink or burned-out light bulbs.

"It doesn't help that I feel like the past year has sucked the intelligence right out of me," I complained to Julie. "I'd better not be getting sick."

I had decisions to make about where the boys and I should live. Soon I would need the energy to pack.

"You know, you have been through a lot," Julie reminded me. "It sounds like you are just exhausted."

She was right; I had been through quite a bit. I was so busy doing what I had to do that I occasionally forgot that some considered my situation hard. I couldn't remember the last time I got a good night's sleep. Concerns woke me at 2:00 a.m. and kept me tossing for hours even as I prayed; something about being on my own kept my mind on high alert. I tried to stick to a healthy diet, but some days I had to remind myself to sit down and eat lunch. I got plenty of exercise thanks to my inability to drive, but my tendency to go until I crashed was catching up with me.

"Why don't you try some vitamins?" Julie suggested. "And I bet you could use more sleep."

Desperate, I called my friend Karen, whom I often went to for her good health advice. She drove me to her favorite health food store. I left with a potent vitamin/mineral supplement and a bottle of flaxseed oil. I justified the cost with reminders that I couldn't afford a virus. I remembered a piece of advice I'd received from another friend after an illness—to think of food as medicine—and thought of the many Bible study lessons that included the verse about our bodies being temples of the Holy Spirit. I forced myself to start going to bed earlier whenever possible. Two weeks later, I had some of my energy back.

Whatever came next, whether that included a move, a new job, or both, I needed to be healthy. God repeatedly sent reminders that I had a responsibility to take care of myself, for my sons' sake and because my body belonged to Him.

As moms we tend to put ourselves last. As single parents under extreme stress, taking care of our physical health can get put on the back burner and take its toll, and at a time when we most need stamina.

Perhaps you've already felt your energy start to tank or paid the price for neglecting your health. Getting enough sleep, spending money on healthy food, and taking time to slow down your frenzied pace may feel selfish, when actually everyone will benefit from your healthy choices. Today, consider your body God's vessel that you need to function well and ask Him how to better care for it.

Lord, forgive me for putting my health at the bottom of my priority list. Help me take better care of myself so I can better care for my kids and my home, do my job well, and endure this challenging time without burning out. Show me how to live more healthfully today. Amen.

TO TAKE INTO YOUR DAY

Read: 1 Corinthians 6:19–20

Consider: How are you feeling physically? How is it affecting your ability to keep up with the demands of your busy life?

Survival Tip: This week do one thing to improve your physical health, whether it's eating better, getting more sleep, taking vitamins, or working off stress through exercise. Note the difference in how you feel.

❁ 35 ❁

One Year Later

You will keep in perfect peace all who trust in you,
all whose thoughts are fixed on you!

Isaiah 26:3 NLT

HAD IT REALLY BEEN A YEAR since my husband left town?

As hard as this anniversary was, it felt strangely empowering.

If I made it through a year, maybe I can do another. I'd rather not have to, but with God's help, I . . . I think I can do this!

Considering the circumstances, I should have been more frustrated than ever. In many ways the boys and I were still in limbo. A strange restlessness had come over me. I felt exhausted, anxious for closure while still struggling to let go of the life we'd lost. Yet I also knew that

God had spent the past twelve months surpassing my expectations and equipping me to do more than anyone thought possible. I had grown in confidence, independence, strength, and dependence on Him. If my husband returned tomorrow, he would be dealing with a different woman than the one he'd left, and this stronger person was the one getting ready to tackle Year Two of single-mom life.

A few days after realizing, *It has been a year*, Nathan and I were once again with family while Christian stayed home to work. Instead of a birthday party at Disneyland, we were enjoying a two-day reunion with my dad's cousins in the town where he and Mom grew up.

While Nathan played water games in the hot July sun, I savored the warmth of connecting with relatives. Maybe it was the fun reunion setting, or being in the city of my birth, or the break from the ordinary, but as I visited and listened to Nathan play in the distance, I dreaded going home. I caught myself talking to my cousin Michelle about rent costs and schools in the area. Dad's cousins and I had nice chats about writing and our kids and a dozen other topics. More than one asked, "Have you considered moving closer to family?"

I heard myself say, "Being here has me thinking about it."

My own words startled me. How could I consider leaving the community that had been home for fourteen years? But the more I pictured the possibilities of a different life, the more free I felt. There was just something about being open to options! I felt a strange peace even though I had no idea if moving would be a good idea, or if my desire only came from the emotional charge of a good time. The peace came from knowing I could trust the God who'd gotten me through the hardest year of my life to show me what to do in the next one.

―――――――――――――

How many times have you cried out to God, *I can't do this*? How has He shown you that, with Him, you can do a lot more than expected? What remarkable things has He done already?

I'm not implying that there is something magical about the One-Year mark. It takes a lot longer than that to adjust and find our bearings. But God often uses anniversaries to awaken our minds to His faithfulness and the strength and determination we've gained by walking a painful path with Him. Not only does time prove that we will make it, but sometimes He opens our minds to possibilities for the next phase that we never would have considered before.

Whether you've made it through your first year as a single mom or your first week, take time to thank God for being with you for every second of it. How do you know you will make it through the next year or the next week?

Lord, I never expected to make it to this point with my sanity intact. You have been so good! Thank You for how You've grown and strengthened me so far. Help me draw on Your track record in moments when I think I can't do this anymore. Thank You in advance for the good You have planned for me and my children, whatever that includes. Amen.

TO TAKE INTO YOUR DAY

Read: Psalm 3:3–5

Consider: How have you grown and changed since you first became a single mom?

Survival Tip: Mark the anniversary on your calendar. Set aside some time on that day to reflect on how far you have come with God's help.

SECTION 5

time to
start over

$\backsim 36 \backsim$

What Should I Do?

If any of you lacks wisdom, you should ask God,
who gives generously to all without finding fault,
and it will be given to you.

James 1:5

THE BANKRUPTCY ATTORNEY'S warning rang in my ears. *"Since you're surrendering the house, bankruptcy will accelerate foreclosure. If I were you, I would move soon."*

A week later, Susan's husband came over to figure out why one of the lights in our dining area wouldn't turn on. He assured me it wasn't a fire hazard but declared it too old to fix and not worth replacing. "Just keep it off. You'll be moving soon."

I'd gone from being thankful to still be in our house to feeling like we were living on a sinking ship. We'd looked at several apartments, none of which were quite right. Christian was prepared to help with rent, but could

I manage when he wanted to move out on his own? Even if I got a full-time job that paid well, child-care costs and taking the bus route into consideration made my head hurt.

Since the reunion I'd felt torn between the family that had wanted to kidnap me and the boys the day my husband sent that life-altering e-mail and the "family" that had carried me through the past year and three months. We had an open invitation to stay with my parents. My attorney had been wise enough to request an option to move early on in the divorce agreement, and my husband didn't fight it. I'd started researching school choices for Nathan in the area where Mom and Dad lived. But how could I uproot us after all we'd lost? Christian didn't want to leave his job, and I didn't want to force him to. Nathan had just started his first year of band.

As I continued to seek God's direction, I watched two friends and their families benefit from a fresh start after losing their homes to foreclosure. Favorite activities suddenly felt like draining chores. I loved my friends but worried that I would never learn to stand on my own with so many moms at my beck and call. I longed for my sons and me to be known for something other than what happened to us. Standing in our now-gloomy house that I'd once shared with a husband, I wondered if my heart would ever heal in the city filled with memories.

I asked a carefully selected group of friends to pray

about my decision. One replied with a list of reasons why moving would be the best thing in the world for us, and another expressed the opposite.

God, what do You *want me to do? Give me wisdom.*

In the end, it came down to the practical. I couldn't afford a decent apartment without putting unfair pressure on Christian. My church family would support me as long as I needed help, but I did not want to make dependency on them a lifestyle.

God was clearly providing the wisdom I'd prayed for. The best thing I could do was trust that He would do the same for Christian and accept the offer of a fresh start.

Becoming a single mom requires tough decisions, including where to live. *Should I fight to stay in the house or find an apartment? Would it be best to stay where everything is familiar or follow an opportunity to start fresh?*

James 1:5 promises that God supplies wisdom for those who ask for it. We need a lot of wisdom as mothers planning for the future. If you aren't wrestling over where to live, you might need clarity for other major decisions. While the prayer support of friends is helpful, only God is capable of seeing to the core of our needs. Ask Him today to set you on the path that is best for you, and for the courage to take it.

Heavenly Father, I don't have the energy for one more decision, but I must make this one, and I don't want to choose the wrong road. Make it clear what is best for us. Help me trust Your plan. Amen.

TO TAKE INTO YOUR DAY

Read: Proverbs 3:5–6

Consider: What do you need God's direction or wisdom for today?

Survival Tip: As you pray over your decision, seek support from friends who will join you in praying for wisdom and clarity rather than tell you what you should do.

37

Crossing the Border

Look straight ahead, and fix your eyes on
what lies before you.
Proverbs 4:25 NLT

I EXPECTED TO CRY through my last Sunday singing
with the choir. Instead, I enjoyed every moment, even as
my heart hurt for what Nathan and I were about to leave:
friends who felt like family, the church where my sons
grew up, Nathan's school, our house, and one precious son.
Christian had decided to stay where his job and friends
were. He had a temporary place to live while he looked
for apartments. During the transition I would homeschool
Nathan using the curriculum from the school he'd attended since kindergarten. They'd even let him keep a donated
trumpet so he could continue practicing until he joined
another school band.

We called what we were doing a trial move, but deep

down I knew better. What good was a fresh start if we turned back?

As the choir led worship songs and sang a special number during the offering, my sister Kristy and my parents waited at the back of the sanctuary. Choir had been the first activity I got involved in when my husband and Christian and I started attending this church fourteen and a half years earlier. How fitting that singing was the last thing I did before leaving town. I'd spent the past two weeks balancing packing with farewell parties. The week before, the pastor prayed for us during the service. After all that, I exited the choir loft only to have friends follow me to where my parents waited. Susan and her family and other friends joined us in the narthex for final hugs, and Julie walked with us to the van and sent me away with a present. What a picture of the love we'd been surrounded by through the trial of our lives.

I remember exactly where we said good-bye to Christian (in the parking lot of the museum where he worked), where we spotted church friends one more time (in our favorite taqueria where we stopped to eat), and the exact moment when Nathan and I crossed the border from one state to the next. My stomach jumped with a mix of sadness and anticipation.

Don't look back, I sensed God telling me. *You're starting a new chapter.* After over a year of living in survival mode, it was time to decompress and rest. We'd been well taken care of by friends, and now my parents and sisters wanted a turn.

By that evening we were at a pizza party to celebrate one of Nathan's cousin's birthdays. Melancholy set in as the sun set, and I thought of the home we'd walked away from, and Christian, and how fragmented life seemed. I looked at Nathan and remembered the feeling of him burying his teary face against my chest after saying good-bye to classmates. Would he be okay? I took a breath and felt God revive the sense of bittersweet release I'd felt while crossing the border. We'd left a lot behind, but maybe we needed to in order to make room for the good plan that we couldn't see yet.

Rebuilding life includes change, and change usually means saying good-bye. You may have already said more than your share of good-byes to friends, family, a job you love, a house full of memories, the life that now seems like a dream. Hopefully you have also discovered benefits, rest, and healing as you allowed God to usher you through a new door. Not everyone has the blessing of going from one support system to another, but when we have the courage to pursue God's next step for us, even if that means leaving security behind, we know we're in loving hands.

"Look straight ahead, and fix your eyes on what lies before you" (Proverbs 4:25 NLT). In what ways do you feel like you're crossing a border? How has embracing change made it possible for you to reconnect with family, recuperate, draw closer to God, or learn to see a little mystery as a good thing?

Lord, thank You for being a Father who has good plans in mind for His children. Help me remember this when I must leave a treasured place for the unknown. Amen.

TO TAKE INTO YOUR DAY

Read: Jeremiah 29:11; Isaiah 55:8–9

Consider: What familiar places or people have you had to leave since becoming a single mom? How has it benefited you?

Survival Tip: Write out a favorite verse that reminds you of God's perfect plan for your future.

38

"I Want to Go Home!"

"Forget the former things; do not dwell on the past.
See, I am doing a new thing! Now it springs up;
do you not perceive it? I am making a way in
the wilderness and streams in the wasteland."

Isaiah 43:18–19

ARRIVAL AT MOM AND DAD'S felt like an episode of one of those home makeover shows. My parents and sisters had spent weeks creating space for Nathan and a bedroom/office for me. They couldn't wait to give us the tour! Nathan's cousins welcomed him like a celebrity. I displayed as many reminders of home as possible. We jumped into our homeschooling routine. Mom and Dad loved having us close; I relished the respite from nonstop stress. I was shocked by how much I needed to sleep and eat. My parents' gated community was a paradise of safety and friendly neighbors.

Then reality sank in. We really had left the life we knew.

"I want to go home!" Nathan burst into tears one evening when move-induced fatigue started to bring out the worst in all of us.

Me too, my heart cried after I saw a picture online of the worship team rehearsing without me.

I locked the door to my bedroom so I could get a grip on my emotions. Was this a mistake? We missed our friends, our church, and Christian. We even missed walking to Walmart.

Was I acting like the Israelites who, before they'd crossed the Red Sea, whined to return to Egypt? Or were we just homesick?

An invitation from Nathan's band teacher back home to play in the Christmas concert came at the perfect time. Before anyone could talk me out of it, I arranged the trip. Nathan spent a day at his old school, and I enjoyed time with friends. Nate and I had two nights with Christian. We hung out in our house and laughed over how it echoed.

There was one thing I didn't do that didn't make sense to anyone, including me. Nathan's concert fell the night before the ladies' Christmas tea at church, but instead of asking someone to squeeze me in, I planned to leave before it started. I knew my friends were upset with me, and I didn't blame them. I wanted to attend. Nathan had plenty of buddies to stay with. We could have spent more time with Christian. Why didn't I stay a little longer?

During the train ride home, the answer came: a beautiful tea at church might have ended with us *really* crying to return to Egypt. Nathan got to play in his concert; we both got to see Christian and our friends. Now it was time to settle in to the new life God had for us. We'd had a wonderful time. We would have plenty of chances to visit and keep in touch, but our hollow house sent the message: *This is no longer your home. It's time for something new.*

Isn't it interesting how quickly we can go from thanking God for a fresh start to wanting the familiar again? Even when the "familiar" was stressful, unhealthy, or impossible to maintain, we want to go back. Familiar is where our friends are, and sometimes where family is. Our kids are sad and homesick. *We* are homesick. We knew what to expect in that familiar place, what was expected of us, and who we were. Did we make a mistake? We know the answer is probably no, but still we cry like the Israelites, "Why did we leave?"

You don't need to have moved to yearn for something or someone you left behind. How kind God is to meet our needs for the people and places we miss even as He tells us,

"See, I am doing a new thing!" (Isaiah 43:19). If you are feeling homesick for your old life, ask God to show you how to ease that ache without going backward. How can you and your children stay connected to the good parts of the past while embracing the new?

Lord, thank You for understanding my homesickness. Show me when it is time to return to a place I love and when it is time to live in the present. Amen.

TO TAKE INTO YOUR DAY

Read: Exodus 14:10–15

Consider: When have you been tempted to go back instead of forward? How has staying in touch with old friends helped? How has it hurt?

Survival Tip: Take a step toward embracing your new life. Meet your neighbors; sign up for an activity; start a new tradition with your kids.

39

A Little Privacy, Please

Very early in the morning, while it was still dark,
Jesus got up, left the house and went off
to a solitary place, where he prayed.

Mark 1:35

NATHAN GRABBED THE KEY to the pool area.

"We'll be back in a while," I told my parents.

For a moment I felt guilty for not inviting them to join me and Nathan in the hot tub, but by then they understood our need for mother/son time.

Unlike the home we left, Mom and Dad's house was a hub of activity. Nathan loved having his cousins and aunts around so often, especially when my sisters popped in during his homeschooling day. Being in a home that wouldn't be snatched out from under us at any time provided much-needed security. After over a year without cable, Nathan enjoyed watching Hallmark movies with Grandma and sports with Grandpa, and I quickly got sucked into *Downton Abbey*. We joined the family for cousins' basketball games, parties, outings, and other fun events we'd missed while living two hundred miles away. Nathan helped Grandpa with projects. We introduced Mom and Dad to new games. But in the evenings I missed quiet times with my sons. The hot tub in Mom and Dad's housing development became a favorite escape. At bedtime, Nathan and I went into my room to read and pray together before I tucked him into his bed in what had once been a sitting area.

If only I could find privacy for myself.

Back home I had solitude as soon as Nathan went to school and Christian left for work. Here I was still learning to juggle homeschooling with freelance work and adjust to a bedroom/office that didn't quite feel like "my writing space" yet. While I'd always been social, the writer in me needed alone time to work and think, hear from God, and process the whirlwind of changes. Where could I find privacy when the house was rarely empty?

I thought about Jesus slipping away to a solitary place. He'd been intentional about finding time alone with His Father. How could I do the same thing?

My bedroom door does have a lock on it. I started to use it. After a while that wasn't enough. I needed a place where no one would knock on my door and activity upstairs didn't distract me. *God, where can I go?*

My love for taking walks led me to some quiet spots in the development, and finally to one secluded bench. If I wanted to be completely alone to think, to pray about something, or to have a private conversation on my cell phone, I went to that bench. If someone else had the same idea, I found one of my backup locations. That special place relaxed my spirit, drew me close to the Lord, and stirred gratitude for His kindness in providing a little privacy.

Like most mothers, you discovered the challenge of finding time alone as soon as you had your first child. Then you became a single mom and it got even harder. Gone are the days when your husband took over while you hibernated in your room or went for a long walk. Being the only parent means less time to spend alone. If you've moved in with family, you are also learning to share space. Is it unrealistic to expect privacy right now? Is it selfish to want it when your kids need you and there is so much to do?

You can use Jesus' example as divine permission. If He needed time away from the crowds and even the friends He loved, we can assume that solitude, especially for time with Him, is a reasonable request. Finding that sacred place and time might require some creativity and searching. But when we seek Him, even for something as personal as alone time, He promises that we will find it.

Lord, I love my kids and the people You've brought into my life, but I also need time to myself. Show me where to find it. Provide a special place for reflection, relaxation, and moments with You. Amen.

TO TAKE INTO YOUR DAY

Read: Matthew 7:8–11

Consider: How has single parenting affected your ability to find privacy?

Survival Tip: Find a place to be alone, even for a few minutes. Take a walk during your lunch hour; get up a half hour earlier to pray and read your Bible; shut yourself in your bedroom after the kids go to sleep. If they are old enough, explain to your children that you need time alone and ask them to respect that time.

40

Not Coming

Rejoice with those who rejoice;
mourn with those who mourn.

Romans 12:15

TO AN OUTSIDER, Nathan might have looked like a ten-year-old overreacting to a small disappointment. But we all knew what he was really crying over. My parents graciously left the room.

I shut the door. "Nate, please calm down." My tears escaped as soon as I hugged him. Why should he calm down? He had every right cry. "I'm so sorry."

His dad had called that morning to say he couldn't come for the weekend after all. He had a horrible virus, so I appreciated him not spreading germs, but this was supposed to be their Christmas visit and Nathan had made big plans. He'd held himself together with his usual good attitude, until an activity with his cousins and uncle didn't work out and sent him over the edge. I felt all the sadness over moving, leaving his brother, and months without seeing his father pour out of him. All I could do was stroke his hair and rub his back and remind him that his dad really did want to come. This wasn't the first time I'd had to console Nathan over a canceled visit, but never before had he reacted with such raw hurt.

God, help me comfort him. Remind him that he's loved.

The past year and a half had taught me and Nathan to get used to plans changing with his dad. Between distance and my ex-husband's work schedule, nothing was guaranteed. It wouldn't do any good to remind Nathan of that. I might need to start waiting until the last minute before telling him, "Your dad is coming to town," but for right now he needed me to let him fall apart.

An hour later, he was worn out from crying but on his way back to being his old self. My sister Kristy called. "Is Nate okay?"

"He'll be all right. I think everything is just catching up with him."

"When I told Ian that Nathan was supposed to see his dad this weekend, he felt awful. He wants to take the kids to the movies tomorrow and then out for burgers . . . It can be a guys' day. Would that be okay?"

"He would love that!" *Thank You, God!*

I knew better than to expect a movie and lunch to

make up for a canceled weekend with Dad; so did Kristy and Ian. But hearing how desperately Ian wanted to help turn Nathan's weekend around, and seeing Nathan perk up when I told him the plan, felt like an embrace from our kind heavenly Father. While I continued to learn how to best comfort my son through days like these, God had me with family members who knew Nathan needed extra care and wanted to give it. When all I could do was hug him and pray for the right words, God had the ability to inspire others to show my son that, even when Dad couldn't be with him, he had a lot of people who loved him.

There is something especially heartbreaking about seeing a child crushed because Dad didn't come through. Whether the reason is valid or not, or expected or not, it still hurts to see anticipation melt into tears. Suddenly all the pat answers we give our children when life doesn't go their way ("Life isn't always fair," "Sometimes things don't work out," "Maybe it happened for a reason") get tossed out the window, and we're left groping for words. All we can do is apply "Mourn with those who mourn" to this sad mother/child moment and cling to the hope that God knows how to comfort better than we do.

Occasionally God shows His care by sending someone to turn the disappointment around; then there are days when we must trust His ability to help our child ride out what can't be fixed. Hopefully every scenario brings us and them one step closer to trusting the One who will always be there.

Heavenly Father, I can't stand to see my child hurt. Give me words of comfort when Dad lets us down. Thank You for knowing how to make up for imperfect people with Your perfect love. Amen.

TO TAKE INTO YOUR DAY

Read: Psalm 103:13–17

Consider: When have you seen God come through after your child's dad didn't?

Survival Tip: Encourage your child to keep a journal, scrapbook, or treasure box of memories of how God cares for them, especially after disappointments.

41

Where My Friends Are

A friend loves at all times,
and a brother is born for a time of adversity.

Proverbs 17:17

I SAT BESIDE DAD'S COUSIN Cheryl feeling like an awkward thirteen-year-old on her first day at a new school. How long had it been since I'd walked into a room filled with women I didn't know? Had it been this scary the last time, or did I just feel vulnerable because of all the baggage I carried in with me? I willed myself to relax. Being here was an answer to prayer; I'd known that the day Cheryl invited me to her Saturday morning Bible study.

Nathan and I had been living at Mom and Dad's house for three months. Only one thing prevented me from feeling content: I missed being with friends on a regular basis. While Nathan had his cousins as companions, I'd left my closest relationships behind. No longer having a husband made girlfriends even more precious. I loved that I got to spend so much time with my sisters and reconnect with old friends, but I longed for a place to belong after so many years of being part of a close community.

Cheryl's friends welcomed me immediately, so why did I feel out of place? I tried to focus on the discussion of the book of Hebrews instead of picturing faces from my Bible study group back home. These women had no idea what brought me here. They didn't know I sang or that I wrote for a living. They didn't know I was a single mom who would soon be divorced, or that I was used to being in an environment where everyone knew at least some of my business. *Wait. They don't know!* How many times had I secretly wanted something like this? Today, I was not the friend who was losing her marriage and her house and couldn't pay her bills. I was Cheryl's cousin Jeanette who'd recently moved back to town. How incredibly freeing!

God instilled a sweet message on my heart that He'd provided a new set of friends for the next chapter of my story. Perhaps there were women in this room whom I needed as God healed me, or maybe one of them needed me. For now it just felt nice to be part of a discussion about the Bible that would not end in me giving an update on my situation, to feel the obvious love in the room, and to sense that I already had a friend in Cheryl.

Saturday mornings became the high point of my week. That was my time for soaking up God's truth, getting to know people over breakfast afterward, hanging out with Dad's cousin, and letting God open my heart to new relationships.

Moving forward after such a major life change tears us away from friends when we are at our loneliest. Some get left behind because of moves; others walk away or phase out of our lives. Sometimes God makes it clear that a fresh start requires a fresh set of friends. Where do we find them? We encourage our kids to reach out; why is it so difficult for us?

As I discovered, the God who filled His Word with evidence that He created us for relationships will not leave us friendless. When we have the courage to be the new girl in the room, sometimes He even reveals benefits in that. He knew exactly who we needed when our hearts were broken, and He knows who we need as our hearts recover. Whether you are missing friends today or feeling restless for a relational do-over, ask God to guide you to the place where your new sisters in Christ are waiting.

Heavenly Father, I really need friends. Thank You for understanding that. Thank You for the friends You have provided already. Show me where to go to find that unique connection that comes from a bond in Your love. Amen.

TO TAKE INTO YOUR DAY

Read: Philippians 1:3–4

Consider: Which friends have you had to say good-bye to? How has God provided for your needs through new relationships?

Survival Tip: Look for an opportunity to connect with people in a fresh way. Join a new Bible study group, get involved in your community, or reach out to women who have similar hobbies.

42

It's Over

Those who know your name trust in you, for you,
LORD, have never forsaken those who seek you.

Psalm 9:10

WHEN THE 9 X 12 ENVELOPE from my attorney's office arrived, I knew what was inside, but my heart still did that weird flippy thing. *I'm not married anymore.*

I'd been waiting for this day of closure. My friend Jan had warned me that seeing the judge's signature on an official divorce decree would feel surreal and strange. She hadn't exaggerated.

Should I tell the kids? From what I could see, the marriage ended for them when their dad moved out. *Not yet. Why drum up unnecessary sadness?*

I e-mailed a few friends with the news but couldn't bring myself to tell anyone out loud for a while. Then I did what Jan said she'd done with her envelope: I stuck it in my file drawer and tried to go on with my day.

I felt free but unsettled, relieved but like I should be grieving. I'd heard about women going out with friends to celebrate when their divorces were final. Should I ask my sisters to take me out? Maybe another day. Or never. I couldn't decide if a party felt appropriate for the occasion, for me anyway. How would Nathan react if I announced, "I'm going out to celebrate being officially divorced"?

My cousin Cheryl suggested that I mark the day by writing about all the things God had done to care for and guide me since my husband left. I took out my journal and wrote a long entry, marveling over how He'd sustained and provided for me and the kids. Still, something was missing from the day. If I didn't feel like rejoicing, shouldn't I be sadder?

Sadder hit six days later as I sat in my Saturday Bible study class feeling the numbness wear off. I managed to keep my emotions to myself until I got to Cheryl's car. Then I dissolved into a puddle of tears right there in the church parking lot.

Did I try hard enough to keep my marriage from crumbling?

Did I love him enough?

Had I really been a good wife? Really?

Would my kids be okay?

We agreed *yes* to all of the above. Then the reality of all the boys and I had lost set in and I cried some more. Cheryl hugged me and prayed for me. Once I'd drained myself of sadness, we went out for breakfast. I guess it was a celebration in a way—a celebration of finally being free to move forward; of God's kindness to me, Christian, and Nathan; of knowing we'd been carried through the crisis of our lives with the help of two loving families, but most of all by Him. I had lost more than my mind could bear to think about, but I also had a wonderful Father at my side as I started to rebuild my life.

If your single-parenting experience has included a long divorce process, you might still be waiting for that moment when it's done. Or maybe it has come already and you're still wrestling with conflicting emotions. *Thank You, God, it's over, finally! But wait. That means . . . it's over. Officially.*

While we ride out the tidal wave of relief and sadness, bouncing between wanting to throw a party and wanting to indulge in a tearjerker film festival, our heavenly Father continues to be faithful. What comfort we have—even with the regret and questions—knowing that verses like Psalm 9:10 have been proven true for us. "Those who know your name trust in you, for you, LORD, have never forsaken those who seek you." The Lord who kept us fed, housed, and stable through our "I can't believe this is my life" past has a future full of good things waiting for us.

Father, sometimes my life still doesn't seem real. But it is, and I don't know how to feel about it. Thank You for being close through the grief and the gratitude. Thank You for carrying me through so much and for the promising future You have in store for me. Amen.

TO TAKE INTO YOUR DAY

Read: Psalm 9:1–2; reread Isaiah 43:18–19

Consider: How has God been faithful to you since you became a single mom? What exciting things is He already starting to do?

Survival Tip: Find a supportive friend to help you through that "It's over" day. Choose someone you feel free to be vulnerable with, who will listen, who will grieve with you, and who will also encourage you to look ahead.

~ 43 ~

Waiting for Boaz

"May the LORD repay you for what you have done.
May you be richly rewarded by the LORD, the God of Israel,
under whose wings you have come to take refuge."

Ruth 2:12

HAD I GONE INSANE? The divorce had been final for only two weeks and I was already thinking about guys. After declaring that I had no interest in dating, I felt ready to go out with anyone who asked.

I finally contacted my friend Jan. She'd warned me where my mind might go.

"What is wrong with me?" I felt so embarrassed.

Jan didn't need me to go into detail. She knew what I was craving. Affection.

"Didn't I tell you?" She let out an *"I've been there"* laugh, like if we were in the same room she would have given me a big hug. "When it happened to me I felt like I was possessed! Trust me, honey. You don't want to go down the road I chose."

I'd heard Jan's story before, but she told me again, about all the regrets her loneliness left her with, including realizing that she'd put her needs for companionship ahead of her kids. She finally had to make a conscious choice for purity for as long as God kept her single. She learned to appreciate time with girlfriends, the freedom to serve at church and enjoy hobbies, and hanging out with male friends in group settings. Most of all she learned to run to Jesus with her need for love and let Him heal her.

"God didn't let me find someone until I craved the arms of Jesus more than I craved the arms of a man."

She told me about her experience reading the book of Ruth. "I told myself I was waiting for Boaz. I hope you'll do the same thing. You don't want less than him."

After twelve years, Jan found her "Boaz." Knowing that filled me with hope.

I hung up determined to wait too. Since my husband had left, I'd gained a new appreciation for Ruth, the young widow who left everything behind to care for her mother-in-law in a foreign land. How many times had I felt like her, alone with nothing to offer but my willingness to work hard? Surely Boaz thought Ruth was beautiful, but he didn't lust after her as she gleaned grain from his fields. His attraction to Ruth's character drove him to want to make her life easier. I couldn't get enough of how Boaz watched out for Ruth and guarded her reputation. Boaz was kind, generous, respectful, and protective—all godly qualities I hoped for in a man. He probably had flaws, but he was exactly what Ruth needed.

I didn't want just any guy; I wanted someone worth waiting for, someone who felt drawn to *me*, not what he wanted from me. While I waited for the Boaz in my life, I prayed that I would run to Jesus like Jan did instead of craving male attention that would only lead to regrets.

Let's be honest; when we have been used to a man's affection, we can miss it no matter what the relationship looked like. It's hard not to be touched, held, and loved. We know better than to crave certain things outside of marriage, but we want them anyway. How could God expect us to live a pure life after all we've been through? But is the scenario in our imagination worth the price?

The story of Ruth and Boaz provides a beautiful example of what God is capable of. Ruth shows us how attractive courage and character are in a woman. She didn't win the heart of a wonderful man by compromising her morals; she won it while doing God's will even in her loneliness.

No matter how desperately you crave the arms of a man today, ask God to make you willing to live as He wants you to as you wait for whomever He has waiting for you.

Lord, I confess that it is hard to keep my desires pure. Help me run to You with my need for affection and love, and take time to heal. Fill my life with lovely examples of what You can do when we are willing to obey You. Amen.

TO TAKE INTO YOUR DAY

Read: Ruth 2

Consider: What do you miss most about having a man in your life? How is Jesus filling those gaps?

Survival Tip: Challenge yourself to read the book of Ruth this week (it's short). Ask God to help you crave more of Him as you wait for His perfectly laid-out plan.

44

Just a Quick Look

No temptation has overtaken you except what is common to
mankind. And God is faithful; he will not let you be tempted
beyond what you can bear. But when you are tempted,
he will also provide a way out so that you can endure it.

1 Corinthians 10:13

I DON'T KNOW WHAT drove me to check my ex-husband's Facebook page. We weren't even "friends." But I did, and he made enough public for me to see his recent status update: "In a Relationship."

The news didn't shock me. Why did it upset me?

He'd included a picture of her, which upset me even more.

I sent an e-mail rant to some friends and took comfort in their assurance that he would never find a woman as high-quality as me.

I showed my sister the photo so she could tell me I was prettier.

This began an unhealthy, junior high-ish obsession with my former husband's relationship status. I knew God had better things for me to do, like work and homeschooling Nathan. But I kept checking for possible updates that I knew would derail me. It hurt to know he'd put the news out there so quickly after the ink dried on our divorce papers. I hated that she was even slightly cute. It seemed unfair that he got to have someone while I did the wise thing and took time to get healthy again. What if he married her? I Googled her name in case she had a criminal record. I Googled his name in case he now had one.

Until one day when I almost literally heard God say, *Stop*.

My ex-husband's dating life was none of my business anymore. He was legally free to be in a relationship. The pressure in my heart and the desire to say snarky things about his choice weren't harming him a bit, but they were doing awful things to my mood. Not to mention that I was wasting time that could be spent with Nathan. What if he walked in on the images of his dad with a girlfriend?

God, help me focus on my own life instead of his.

"I'm done stalking his Facebook page," I told two friends.

They promised to hold me accountable.

My decision didn't double as a quick fix. I had to remind myself daily that this was an exercise in self-discipline. I slipped up often. *What worthwhile thing should I be doing instead?* became my go-to question when temptation hit.

The next relationship update came through Nathan after his dad introduced him to his girlfriend and her daughter during a visit. I waited for him to be upset about it. He wasn't. She was a nice lady and he'd had fun playing laser tag with her daughter. Now I faced a new challenge of balancing what was my business (how his dad's relationships affected Nathan) and what wasn't (whether or not I approved).

When the urge to check gripped me again, I blocked my ex-husband's Facebook page for a while so I was no longer able to take even a quick look.

It's a sobering moment when we realize that a person we once shared a life with is now free to pursue other women. The part of us that expected to be one for life still wants to know what he's up to. Then we find out and wish we'd never snooped. How do we respond when we hear God lovingly telling us that it's time to stop letting our curiosity win?

"No temptation has overtaken you except what is common to mankind . . ." Until my battle over my ex-husband's Facebook update, I had applied 1 Corinthians 10:13 to the obvious sins, not the bad habits that robbed me of peace, time, and movement forward. When we recognize our fixation as one more common temptation, and that we really do have some power over it, we make it possible for God to show us the way out.

Lord, I don't know why I want to know what he's doing when finding out wounds me. Show me what to keep track of for my children's sake and what to categorize as none of my business. Thank You for providing escapes when I chose to be disciplined. Amen.

TO TAKE INTO YOUR DAY

Read: Hebrews 4:14–16

Consider: When has your curiosity gotten you into trouble?

Survival Tip: Ask at least one close friend to hold you accountable to stop obsessing about what is no longer your business.

45

A Bittersweet Call

*For I am confident of this very thing, that He who
began a good work in you will perfect it
until the day of Christ Jesus.*

Philippians 1:6 NASB

IT HAD BEEN MONTHS since Christian sounded this
excited, so when he told me, "I signed a lease on an apartment," I forced myself to share his joy.

"That's great. Where is it?"

He described the location and told me about the room-
mate he'd found at work. My heart leapt then fell, one
minute proud of him for taking this step into adulthood
and the next disappointed. Nathan and I and my entire ex-
tended family had been praying that loneliness would draw
Christian "home." We'd made it clear that he was welcome.
In the end he'd decided to stay put. At his age I probably
would have chosen a secure job and friends over family too.

He liked his work. He'd even gotten a raise. Did I expect him to live with me forever?

Nathan seemed to understand his brother's decision better than I did. "He can't exactly quit his job. That would be pretty irresponsible, Mom."

"Not really," I argued. "He could use a fresh start too."

The thought of Christian being alone and away from family had haunted me since the day we parted in the museum parking lot.

He chose to stay.

It still felt wrong. My sons and I had always been close. All those months of only them and me had tightened our bond even more. I wanted what was left of my broken family together again.

Something that friends had told me many times replayed in my mind: *"He's not a kid; he's a man."* Was I holding him back from being one?

For a year and a half, Christian had accepted the role of man of the house that never should have been his. He'd cared for Nathan, fixed the back fence, sprayed for spiders, installed new doorknobs, chased after our crazy dog, and bought his share of groceries. Instead of hanging out with friends at night, he'd often helped make dinner and played board games with his mom and little brother. In some ways our crisis postponed his launch into adulthood; in other ways it equipped him. He was ready to have an apartment with friends. No matter how desperately I wanted my son close, he needed to spread his wings and become who God had created him to be. Someday Nathan would be ready to move out too, and I wouldn't want to stop him either.

As I tried to make sense of what felt like one more loss, I thanked God for providing me with a generous, thoughtful, obedient older son who picked up the slack for a long time. It was time to see what great purpose God had in mind for him, even if I had to do that through tears and wishing things could be different.

———

Raising our kids alone ties us to them in a unique way. It is easy to become dependent on their help and companionship and hold them back from steps of growth. We know in our hearts that God did not give us children so they could stick around for life, or to be our source of security while they're still under our roof. So why do rites of passage feel like cruel losses, or even rejection?

You might be years away from the day when your child leaves home. Until then, what milestones have you been wrestling against while God gently urged you to let go? What wonderful things do you see Him doing in your son or daughter that you do not want to selfishly hold him or her back from? How are you allowing God to prepare you to live without your kids so you can each fulfill the good work He has started?

Lord, forgive me for holding my children too tightly at times. Thank You for using sad circumstances to draw us closer as a family. Help me remember that my kids were still only given to me for a little while. Help me encourage their steps of independence even as I struggle to let go. Amen.

TO TAKE INTO YOUR DAY

Read: Proverbs 3:1–4; 22:6

Consider: How have you grown closer to your children since becoming a single mom? How will this make it harder to let go when it's time?

Survival Tip: List a few benefits to allowing your kids to grow up.

SECTION 6

a beautiful thing

46

A Place to Be Sad

Jesus wept.

John 11:35

THE FEELING THAT I'd forgotten to do something important hit after the divorce papers arrived and nagged at me through the summer. What had I left out?

We felt settled at Mom and Dad's.

Nathan was enrolled in public school.

We'd found a church and friends.

I no longer had divorce or bankruptcy hanging over my head.

Christian had a place to live.

What hadn't I done?

You didn't grieve.

I brushed the thought aside. *Sure I did.* I'd cried with Cheryl. I let myself be vulnerable with my Saturday morning Bible study group. Before moving I shed plenty of tears.

Why did I still feel like I'd skipped a step, and like moving forward and being the mom that Nathan needed depended on it?

You must deal with all of the loss and pain. It's time.

That thought replayed in my mind whenever I told someone why we moved and realized I felt shaky.

I guess I'd never let the magnitude of all that had happened sink in. I'd been too busy surviving. Friends were shocked when they heard that I'd gone through so much without counseling or attending a support group. I'd never felt a need for any of that. Or maybe I just wasn't ready until now. I knew Jesus bore every burden with me, and I'd learned to lean on Him like never before, but I sensed even He was nudging me to take time to feel something. The trouble was, I had no idea what I needed.

Lord, show me what will help, I prayed silently one morning during Bible study.

I remembered a scene from a movie I'd watched years earlier, about a group of friends that gathers for a reunion at the camp where they'd met as teenagers. One friend was missing, but his widow showed up.

"Why did you come?" someone finally had the courage to ask.

"Because I needed to be sad."

I think that's what I need.

I knew I'd found my place to be sad when I sat in the

third session of a class for women who'd been down the same road that brought me back to my parents' house. We'd just divided into small groups. This was the night for sharing our stories. One woman after another poured out tales that echoed mine. The lump in my throat grew with each one. When my turn came I barely got out two words.

"This is the place to let out your feelings." My small group leader's soothing counselor-like voice broke the dam.

A lady across from me who'd just finished crying handed me the tissues.

As awkward as it felt to sit there weeping in front of people I'd barely met, I knew I'd found a refuge. In this room filled with women who'd survived the journey, I could finally make sense of all that had happened, give myself permission to be devastated over it, and let the Lord who understood grief heal my heart.

With all we have to do as busy moms, healing can get pushed to the back burner. If we stopped for every rush of sadness, anger, regret, and loss, we'd never get through the day. Eventually, though, all we've been pushing back for the sake of survival catches up with us and we need to find a place to release our grief before it eats us alive.

If Jesus allowed Himself to grieve when His friend Lazarus died—and in public—we can mourn what we've lost too. But where do we begin? Where is that safe place away from the kids and the mountain of responsibility? You might be searching for your place to be sad right now. Do you need a counselor? A support group? Both? Ask God to show you what you need and to be your Source of comfort until you find a resource that is perfect for you.

Lord, I needed to live in survival mode for a while. Now I need to be sad. Thank You for carrying my grief and being kind enough to also let Yourself experience it. Give me the courage to face the painful journey of healing, knowing You will be with me. Amen.

TO TAKE INTO YOUR DAY

Read: Isaiah 53:4–6; John 11:17–36

Consider: How have you dealt with your grief? What have you postponed or avoided?

Survival Tip: If you are still looking for your place to be sad, ask some other single moms what helped them.

47

Ring of Truth

The LORD appeared to us in the past, saying:
"I have loved you with an everlasting love;
I have drawn you with unfailing kindness."

Jeremiah 31:3

"WHAT A PRETTY RING." My friend examined the sterling silver ring on my left hand.

"I bought it before moving." I blushed, hoping my explanation wouldn't come across as pitiful. "It's my reminder that I'm still valuable."

She squeezed my hand. "That's beautiful. And you *are* valuable, by the way. Don't forget that."

A month before packing the U-Haul to move, I'd felt a desire to replace the emerald that had served as a covering against feeling naked without a wedding ring. I wanted something meaningful to take into the next stage of life. I knew exactly how I would pay for it.

Shortly after my husband moved out, I'd started receiving occasional cards from a friend I'd met at a writers' conference. Each one included a small amount of cash and an uplifting note. *I know this isn't much, but I wanted to remind you how valuable you are.* How could I put that toward groceries or the phone bill? I'd stashed the money away, hoping to someday make a purchase like this.

My friend Kathy and I planned a special shopping trip to find a ring. I had no idea what I was looking for, only that I wanted sterling silver and it needed to be unique. A silver crown with a cross in the center caught my eye immediately. I tried not to like what appeared to be a representation of the "You're God's Princess" theme. But it showed up in the second shop too, and I kept coming back to it, holding it up, and trying it on. *I wanted to remind you how valuable you are.*

I told Kathy about my friend's cards. God had used her notes to remind me of a truth that reflected my position in His eyes. I'd accepted Jesus as my Savior as a little girl; over this past year leaning on Him in a deeper way allowed me to experience what it meant to be cared for by the King of the universe. "I think this is the one."

"You keep coming back to it, so it must be."

In moments when my ex-husband's choice left me feeling worthless, that ring continued to remind me of the truth.

One evening I decided to show it to the ladies in my support group. They passed it around. "What a great idea." I still forgot the ring's meaning sometimes, but running my fingers over that crown and cross, and remembering buying it with Kathy using five-, ten-, and twenty-dollar bills that always seemed to arrive when I needed a lift, brought me back to reality. *"I have loved you with an everlasting love . . ."* I knew those words were true.

How have the circumstances that led to you becoming a single mom squelched your sense of value? How many times have you read truths in His Word, only to have the lack of a wedding ring and a heart reeling from loss and memories tell you differently? "I have loved you with an everlasting love"—how many times have you had to choose to accept the truth in Jeremiah 31:3 long before your heart believed it?

Then again, how has God used friends, perfectly timed cards, e-mails, or text messages, and moments with Him to remind you how valuable you really are? How has your journey as a single mom drawn you closer to the One who values you more than any human could? As you let your heavenly Father's message, "I have loved you with an everlasting love," sink in, reflect on how He has made that love real to you. How can you memorialize His love and your value in His eyes for moments when you need a refresher?

Heavenly Father, forgive me for allowing the dark side of my story to hold me back from believing the truth that I am loved. Thank You for sending reminders of my value when I need them. Amen.

TO TAKE INTO YOUR DAY

Read: Psalm 23; 1 Peter 2:9

Consider: Who has God used to remind you that you're valuable? How have you learned this through His care for you?

Survival Tip: Consider buying something to remind you of your worth in God's eyes (a ring, a necklace, a plaque, or something else that you know you'll treasure).

48

Family Photos

The Lord is my strength and my shield;
my heart trusts in him, and he helps me.
My heart leaps for joy, and with my song I praise him.
Psalm 28:7

NATHAN'S COUSINS JUMPED INTO the deep end of the pool. Nathan made his way along the edge from the shallow side. My spirit wilted over his lack of swimming experience. In two months he would go to camp with a friend from his old school. Why hadn't I figured out a way to give him more than one session of swim lessons two summers ago? Why had I allowed scenes from *Jaws* to kill my confidence in the water and my ability to be a better teacher myself? Where was his dad at a time like this? My fears of Nathan being messed up forever were coming true. He would be the only boy at camp who couldn't leave the shallow end.

"I bet Ian will work with him," Kristy whispered to me.

She hopped up from her lounge chair. Three minutes later, I heard her husband's laid-back voice coaxing Nathan away from the edge. Nathan linked his arms with Ian's. By the time we were ready to have the kids dry off, Nathan was dunking himself, touching the bottom of the deep end, and attempting strokes on his own.

"Good job, Nate." One of his cousins threw him a towel.

If only I'd had my camera. Instead, I said a prayer of thanks to God for sending Ian to make up for a skill that I lacked. Nathan didn't have a father close by to teach him how to swim, but he had patient relatives. We had come here trusting that God had a purpose for us leaving the familiar behind. I had just witnessed a reward of obeying His nudge toward family.

In my bedroom I had some pictures that I regularly shared with friends—shots of our first holiday season after the move, day trips, me with my sisters, Nate hanging Christmas lights with Grandpa, Uncle Brandon giving Nate a drum lesson. In some Nate looked like a displaced little boy, but a cousin usually had a loving arm draped around him. My favorite picture showed Nathan and my sister Sherry's two youngest kids sharing a group hug with Grandpa. Nathan smiled into the camera, his head against Grandpa's chest, secure and content. He had lost so much, but he knew he was with people who loved him. Whenever I questioned my choice to move I looked at that picture. God had sent us to a place where we could relax and catch up on life, including mastering swimming. For the first time in a very long time, our lives felt almost . . . normal. Nathan had great role models through uncles, aunts, and grandparents, and cousins he adored and fought with like siblings. I had my sisters to add to a new bunch of friends and a growing list of reasons to thank God.

When we make a change out of necessity, we might not expect to see blessings on the other side. If we can breathe a sigh of relief knowing we didn't make a huge mistake, that alone is a reason to praise God. But it is often these changes that lead to beautiful advantages for our kids, and even for us. Moving closer to family can provide security, help that wasn't available before, and role models. Or maybe you've gained through restarting your life in an apartment complex filled with other mothers and children. Whichever changes you've had to make, and regardless of how things look at this moment, ask God to give you a reason to say, "My heart leaps for joy, and with my song I praise him" (Psalm 28:7). Ask Him to begin showing you why He inspired or allowed you to be right where you are.

Father, thank You for revealing so many benefits of stepping out in faith and trusting You. Thank You for meeting my needs and my kids' needs, and revealing Your closeness and love wherever we go. Amen.

TO TAKE INTO YOUR DAY

Read: Psalm 28:6–9; 138:1–3
Consider: How has God used difficult changes to provide for your needs?
Survival Tip: Collect reminders of God's faithfulness as you move forward—pictures of your happy children, good report cards, certificates for activities that your kids finally got to participate in . . .

49

Silliness, Sanity, and Other Gifts

A cheerful heart is good medicine,
but a crushed spirit dries up the bones.

Proverbs 17:22

"I KNEW I WAS HEALING when I got my sense of humor back," a woman in my support group said.

The ladies around me nodded.

I kept quiet. Was there something wrong with me?

What would happen if I shared, "I never lost my sense of humor"? Did that reflect serious denial issues?

Since my husband left, the verse about God keeping our tears in a bottle had seemed like a gross understatement. *More like a ten-gallon drum!* But I'd also laughed a lot. At times I could be guilty of covering my hurt with humor, but my joy was usually sincere. I didn't appreciate it if a friend tried to make me laugh when I felt like crying;

however, if tears naturally morphed into fits of laughter, I found it refreshing.

Wit ran deep in the roots of my family tree, and both boys had inherited it. If I overheard Nathan's deep belly laugh, I cracked up before I knew what was funny. Christian's impression of Napoleon Dynamite could pull me out of the deepest funk. Memories of game nights with the boys included few serious moments. I still laughed when I remembered them ganging up on me while playing Uno; Christian buying all the cheap properties on the Monopoly board, then loading them with hotels so he could oppress the poor; and a Clue game coming to a halt over my question, "If the guy who owns this mansion could afford an observatory and a theater, where is the bathroom?"

Was it normal for a mother and two sons who were about to lose their home to be so silly? Should I have received comments like, "You radiate joy today"? Was it natural for a woman who'd once had to make a conscious decision not to fall back into depressive patterns to be the only one in the room who didn't have to wait for the return of her sense of humor? It seemed almost *super*natural.

It's a gift, I realized. *A cheerful heart is good medicine.*

I relaxed into the knowledge that there was nothing wrong with me. God had made it possible to live the truth behind the proverb. While my heart had been crushed, He'd provided regular doses of fun to keep my bones from drying up completely. Without a sense of humor and an ability to goof off with my kids, I might not have been able to fight off depression and be the mother they needed. A lack of laughter in the home might have dragged their spirits down. I was still working on getting my brain back, and it had taken a while to restore my energy, but I felt more physically healthy than I had in years. Christian and Nathan were pictures of health too.

Losing my marriage and my home hadn't made me happy. It inflicted deep wounds, and grief still hit when I least expected it. But joy in suffering continued to be one of God's sweetest gifts.

The events that create single moms are anything but joyful. How could we possibly be expected to laugh with so many reasons to cry? You may have experienced days when you wondered if you would ever smile without faking it again. Then you catch yourself laughing and experience the healing power of a cheerful heart.

What a wonderful thing God provided when He created humans with the ability to laugh, joke, have fun, and see the humor hidden in an otherwise sad day. Verses like Proverbs 17:22, "A cheerful heart is good medicine, but a crushed spirit dries up the bones," remind us that we need joy to survive. If you are still waiting to get your sense of humor back, ask God to send you a moment of laughter today, whether it's through your children, through a friend, or while enjoying our Creator's sense of fun reflected in nature. Capture every moment of joy as a treasure.

Lord, it doesn't make sense to laugh when I have so much to be sad about. But if I go without it for too long, my spirit will shrivel up. Thank You for the moments of humor that come when I need them. Give me a cheerful heart today. Amen.

TO TAKE INTO YOUR DAY

Read: Psalm 16:5–11
Consider: What brings you joy?
Survival Tip: Do one thing this week that will make you smile or laugh.

∽ 50 ∾

"I'm a Single Mom Too"

As iron sharpens iron, so one person sharpens another.

Proverbs 27:17

CHERYL, SARA, ROBIN, AND I found a table on the patio of the funky downtown café. Sara had just joined our Bible study, and Robin was enjoying a rare morning when she could spare time for breakfast instead of getting home to her kids or chores. As we sipped our coffee and waited for our food to arrive, I looked around the table and realized that Cheryl was the only one of us who didn't fall into the *single mom* category.

Lately God had been bringing woman after woman into my life who happened to be going through a divorce and/or were raising kids alone. Between my support group and Bible study friends, I'd encountered some who were just starting the long, awful road and others who were still waiting for never-ending processes to free them to move on. Some shared their kids equally with Dad; others had situations similar to mine. Our backstories were sadly similar, which broke my heart while also stirring deep empathy. God clearly knew we needed one another. If I saw one of these women wiping away tears and repressing sobs, I couldn't *not* offer comfort; if I overheard a lady mention she was going through a divorce, I wanted to invite her out for coffee or a walk, or encourage her to e-mail me. How many times had I said, "I'm a single mom too" since moving back to Mom and Dad's?

On that lovely spring morning at the café, I knew God had arranged the time especially for the four of us. Cheryl sat back and listened to me, Sara, and Robin share parts of our stories with one another, exchange wisdom and prayer needs, and verbalize frustrations and fears. Two of us were adjusting to living with our parents again. Sara and Robin were both in the throes of steps that I'd finished. And Cheryl was our mutual big sister, eager to pray for and support each of us even though she'd never been in our shoes. We talked long after we'd taken our last bites and noticed we'd let our coffee get cold, the entire time sensing the sweet presence of the Lord that brought us together and was faithfully sustaining each of us.

If not for the events of the past couple of years, I wouldn't have found these remarkable women. I'd never had a single mom as a close friend until I became one. Back home, God arranged for me and Nancy to support each other. Now He was drawing Sara, Robin, and others to me with a magnetic force. While learning from their examples, I saw myself entering a stage where others were learning from mine as well. We could pray for, encourage, and sustain one another in ways that only one who has been there can.

———————

Once we've been through an experience that changes us, God has an interesting pattern of bringing people into our lives who are on the same path. There is something uniquely sweet about connecting with women who share our faith and also understand the tsunami of emotions, change, and ongoing procedures that come with seeing one life crumble while struggling to build a new one. When these special heart connections happen, we understand how it is possible that friendship could be compared to iron sharpening iron. These are the relationships where support is given and received at the same time, and we all come out stronger and better. Even brief encounters when we have the privilege of sharing a struggling mom's hurt can feel like God-ordained moments.

Proverbs 27:17 says, "As iron sharpens iron, so one person sharpens another." How has God made this a reality in your life through new relationships? How has He used other single moms to sharpen you (and vice versa) in ways that other friends can't?

Lord, thank You for the other single moms whom You have brought into my life. Remind me to pray for these friends and their children. Encourage them today, Lord. Amen.

TO TAKE INTO YOUR DAY

Read: Proverbs 18:24

Consider: How many single moms did you know before you became one? How many do you know now?

Survival Tip: Plan a time to hang out with another single mom. Take a walk, take your kids to the park to play while you chat, or get coffee. How are your situations similar? How can you pray for each other?

$\backsim$ 51 $\backsim$

Because I Get It

Praise be to the God and Father of our Lord Jesus Christ,
the Father of compassion and the God of all comfort,
who comforts us in all our troubles, so that
we can comfort those in any trouble with
the comfort we ourselves receive from God.

2 Corinthians 1:3–4

MY BIBLE STUDY FRIENDS sat around a table brainstorming some possible service projects. When it came to planning, I usually let the stronger personalities take charge. But the longer we talked, the stronger tug I felt to suggest what came to mind when someone mentioned holiday-related ideas.

Before I lost my nerve I blurted out, "How about Valentine's Day? That's a hard day for single women." I'd learned this the first time I went shopping for Valentine treats for the boys and cards for Nate's class and realized

I no longer had a sweetheart to buy for. I would not get a heart-covered card, flowers, chocolate, or a pretty present . . . for the first time in over two decades. As if a lack of romance wasn't enough of a reason to dread the holiday, my husband and I had gotten engaged on Valentine's Day. It was all I could do to grab what I needed and get out of Walmart.

I told my new friends the story of how God had restored the holiday for me.

I survived my first husband-less Valentine's Day thanks to Julie. When the day came, I admitted to her, "I just want to get today over with." A few hours later, she showed up at my door with a big heart-shaped box of chocolates and a card. I could still hear her sweet "Happy Valentine's Day" and see her warm smile. The card included a note about how special I was to God and to her. She could have easily dismissed my angst with, "Oh, honey, it's just a day." Instead, she reminded me that I mattered.

"It would be nice to do that for other women."

The idea took off.

We decided to make goodie bags filled with treats, beaded bracelets that my niece and I had made for her school leadership project, and love notes from Jesus. The majority of the bags went to our church's Divorce Care class, but the women got so excited buying goodies that we also had enough for a women's shelter and another ministry.

I overflowed with joy as our group filled the bags. For a very long time I'd been on the receiving end of kindness. This was my chance to comfort complete strangers whose pain I couldn't possibly understand until I did understand. Nothing in the bag was fancy or expensive, but I prayed that each woman would feel God's love as profoundly as I did when Julie had shown up at my door.

"Praise be to the God and Father of our Lord Jesus Christ, the Father of compassion and the God of all comfort, who comforts us in all our troubles, so that we can comfort those in any trouble with the comfort we ourselves receive from God" (2 Corinthians 1:3–4). The road to where you are now has probably included more emotional pain than you thought you could bear. But I bet it has also filled you with compassion that can only come from suffering, and a desire to offer the same comfort to others that you have received, or wished you'd received.

As you get a bit closer to the other side of pain, thank God for the opportunities you have to pass whatever got you through difficult days on to others. It is unlikely that you will allow another single mom to hurt alone. After all you've experienced, you will be the first to give a hug, send a card, offer help, or reach out with a tangible expression of God's love.

Lord, thank You for the friends who took time to remind me I was worth remembering on days when I would have missed out. May I never forget what it felt like to dread a day or event, or the comfort of having that same day or event made better by an act of kindness. Amen.

TO TAKE INTO YOUR DAY

Read: 2 Corinthians 1:3–7

Consider: How has God's kindness increased your compassion and heart for others?

Survival Tip: Reach out to someone who is hurting in a way that you once hurt. How can you remind her that she is valued by God and others?

52

My Not-So-Pathetic Life

Now all glory to God, who is able, through his mighty power
at work within us, to accomplish infinitely
more than we might ask or think.

Ephesians 3:20 NLT

"IT JUST HIT ME how pathetic my life must look," I told Cheryl. "I am now divorced, bankrupt, and living with my parents. Throw legally blind in there and . . . why don't you hand me a tin cup and drop me off on a street corner somewhere?"

We laughed, but even as the words came out of my mouth, I knew the exact opposite was true. The scenes from my life could inspire a sappy TV movie. I'd gone from being a wife to a divorced woman. My belongings had been reduced to what I could fit in my bedroom, a corner of my parents' garage, and a 10 x 10 storage unit that would need to be emptied soon. I was still trying to find my place in a church much larger than the tight-knit one I'd left. I had one son with me and another two hundred miles away. While my freelance work was steady, I barely earned enough to support myself and Nathan. Emotional bumps in the road continued to remind me that healing would require more than one fourteen-week support class. Even with all of the above being true, God had kept His promise from Psalm 27:13: "I would have despaired unless I had believed that I would see the goodness of the LORD in the land of the living" (NASB).

All I had to do was glance up at the top shelf of my closet, where I kept what I called my Blessings Box. It overflowed with reminders that every step of this journey had been walked with a faithful Lord, friends, and family who modeled Christlike love. The box held the cards from our 12 Days of Christmas gift, the notes that once contained cash that had purchased my silver crown-and-cross ring, a vintage handkerchief that a dear friend sent "for your precious tears," and so many other mementoes that I could barely keep it shut.

Sure, Nathan and I lived with my parents and might for a long time, but it had provided us with a much-needed sense of family and freed me to regroup and discover what God had in mind next. How could I call any of that pathetic?

"Maybe it's time to start a new box," Cheryl suggested.

We found one that looked perfect. It was covered with butterflies. The word *Dream* swept across the front. Did I dare do what it said? While standing in line to purchase it, I spotted a spiral journal that gave me the courage. On the front a spunky-looking girl rested one hand on her hip and the other on the words, *At any given moment you have the power to say this is NOT the way this story is going to end.*

I snatched up that journal knowing I had no idea how my story would end, or how Christian's or Nathan's would end. But the God who continued to let me see His goodness knew and had already proven Himself able to do more than I could dream up.

What does your life look like now compared to the day you started this journey? What prayers are you still waiting for God to answer? What have you gained? How have you changed for the better? How has God drawn you closer to Himself?

It's easy to get swept away into the land of the lost and only see what we wish could be different. When we hold on to the reminders of all the good God has done in the process, we begin to see the beauty in our story. When we start to doubt His willingness to fulfill Ephesians 3:20 in our lives and do more than we ask or think, we can reflect on the many ways that He has already proven Himself faithful.

As you sort through the past and find the courage to hope for a much brighter future, may God send you daily reminders of His goodness as you look forward to the beautiful life He has planned for you.

Heavenly Father, thank You for never leaving my side through this heartbreaking time. Thank You for the countless ways that You have been good, kind, and loving. Let me continue to experience Your nearness as I trust You with my future. Amen.

TO TAKE INTO YOUR DAY

Read: Ephesians 3:16–21; reread Psalm 27:13
Consider: How has God allowed you to see His goodness as you adjusted to being a single mom? In what ways has your relationship with Him deepened?
Survival Tip: Gather a few mementoes of God's kindness to you. Buy or make a pretty box to keep them in.

Acknowledgments

As a teenager and young adult, I dreamed of acting and one day giving an Oscar speech, tearfully thanking everyone who "made this possible." This is so much more exciting than that! God knew how to best use my desire to create and communicate—through writing that reflects His goodness. What a privilege!

I am so grateful to the wonderful people He surrounded me with as I wrote this book. Thank you to my wonderful agent and friend, Wendy Lawton, for making me part of the Books & Such family just when I needed a boost of confidence. You believed in my writing, kindly nurtured me as I got my career going again after a long dry spell, and found the perfect home for *Suddenly Single Mom*. I love that I got to know you as a friend and sister in Christ long before becoming your client. You are a gem, "cousin."

I will never stop thanking God for the Mount Hermon Christian Writers' Conference, where I found my place to "fit," grew up as a writer, have met valued friends and mentors (including Wendy), and always connect with Him in profound ways. Every year feels like a family reunion.

Thank you to everyone at Worthy Inspired, especially Pamela Clements, their incredible associate publisher whom I had the honor of calling my editor. Your excitement over this project and constant encouragement mean so much to me!

To everyone who prayed for me: Xochi, my precious Monday morning prayer partner; my friends Marilyn, Julie, Susy, Kay, Margaret, Cheryl, and Heidi; the choir and worship team at Community Presbyterian Church; the Inspire Castro Valley Critique Group; the Pen-Souls prayer group; the ladies in my Saturday morning Bible study; and so many other friends and family members—thank you for reading and/or listening to my sometimes-lengthy updates, sharing my praises, allowing me to also pray for you, and supporting me as I wrote a book that required reliving the past.

Mom, Dad, and Nathan: Thanks for understanding when I lived behind a closed door all day. You were so sweet not to take it personally when I hid my work-in-progress as soon as you came in the room. Thank you for celebrating every milestone with me. I am truly blessed!

Christian and Nathan: My story included your stories, and you allowed me to share so openly. That is such an example of what amazing young men you both are. I love you guys more than I can express without embarrassing you publicly.

Though I didn't specifically name the church I attended or the city I lived in when I first became a single mom, I hope the friends I knew there understand how deeply I treasure them. My memory is filled with more stories of your kindness and love than I could possibly include in one book. I thank God for each of you!

Finally, thank You, Lord, for this painful, beautiful, life-altering journey. You know exactly what each of us needs in order to become the person You had in mind when You created us. Thank You for walking every step of this path with me, and for continuing to use it for Your glory.

JEANETTE HANSCOME is an author, writing teacher, speaker, and busy mom. Her work has been featured by Focus on the Family, Standard Publishing, Walk Thru the Bible, and Lifeway. She enjoys cooking, knitting, reading, studying the Bible, and spending time with her two incredible sons. Jeanette was born with a rare vision disorder called achromatopsia, which means she has no color vision, is extremely light-sensitive, and has visual acuity in the legally blind range. Jeanette lives in the San Francisco Bay Area.

jeanettehanscome.com

IF YOU ENJOYED THIS BOOK, WILL YOU CONSIDER SHARING THE MESSAGE WITH OTHERS?

Mention the book in a blog post or through Facebook, Twitter, Pinterest, or upload a picture through Instagram.

Recommend this book to those in your small group, book club, workplace, and classes.

Connect with Jeanette at facebook.com/ AuthorJeanetteHanscome and post a comment or photo.

Tweet "I recommend reading #SuddenlySingleMom by @ JHanscomeWriter // @worthypub"

Pick up a copy for someone who would be challenged and encouraged by this message.